Along Life's Road

Book 1

Poetry, Songs and Stories

Written By Albert E. Vicent
Compiled By Haruka Vicent
And Michael Vicent
Cover Photo By Albert C. Vicent

Order this book online at www.trafford.com
or email orders@trafford.com

Most Trafford titles are also available at major online book retailers.

Print information available on the last page.

ISBN: 978-1-4907-7092-5 (sc)
ISBN: 978-1-4907-7091-8 (e)

Trafford rev. 03/11/2016

www.trafford.com

North America & international
toll-free: 1 888 232 4444 (USA & Canada)
fax: 812 355 4082

Life's Road

Along Life's Road
There's rocks, small large
Of assorted size
There's worn spots thru
Deep, lengthy, to smooth
Green grass,
Trees of green-
Along the sides
The road smoothes too
As up it climbs
Toward sky of blue
White drifting clouds
Sunshine,
And memories too
Along life's road..
As you travel-on it,
Thru.

Poems

In Love

The light that
Shines the brightest
Seems to be the one
That's most far from reach.
Because the closer
We come to it
The farther away
It seems we are.
And the greater lesson
It seems to teach-
In love, patience, ...and
Glowing light-
To reach.

Hear It

Hear it-
Moving round the house
Rattling doors
Moving window screens
Blowing grass
Moving leaves
Shaking trees
Moving clouds-
On high
Just whistling…
Hear it-
Chase the wind
And tell it…
Hi.

Be Bold

Be bold
Comes from old
There's power-there's magic in it
Don't be afraid
Let em know you're there
They won't be aware
Maybe you don't know too.
Be bold-
Same as you're told
Be who you are
True-good when you do
You'll get thru
Be bold-…
Comes from old.

Stars

Reach for the stars
Reach a little higher
Each day.
It doesn't matter
If you arrive
Night or day.
If you reach
And reach
A little each day
To reach the stars
From where-
You are
much
Can be done
In that way-just reach.

The Door

When you leave
Leave soft-
Just close the door
And be off-
To where-
You've never been before
We'll understand
We won't like it tho
For we don't want,
To see you go.
We love you here
And always will
We'll never forget you
It will be so still.
But… if it's the time
For you to go.
When you leave
Leave soft-
Just close the door
And be off
To where-you've never been before
And always know
Our love is with you
Wherever you,
Will ever-go

All Day

Up the road
Over the hill
That's where all.
The good things stay.
Like little cozy houses
With quaintly twisted roofs
And small cute ponds
Where bull frogs croak
Where the sun shines bright
About all day
And clouds just drift
Then melt away.
Skies stay blue
About all day-just for you.
Up the road-over the hill
That's where all the good things stay
Watched by fairies-
And elves, all day.

Nice

Ice cold rice
Cold cold ice
Rice and ice
And ice and mice
Oh I like rice
Rice is nice,

One Little Fly

One little
It-see
Bit-see
Tiny little fly
Flying very quiet
In the great big sky.
Just where did it go
I really don't know
But it flew by here
A long ti-me
Ago.

Golly Gee

It's a real nice day
Kind of hot too
The sun's shining bright
I don't feel just right
Because I'm three years old
And I'm four today
And I really want to play
Get a little dirty
Its more fun that way.
I can't cause I'm all dressed up
Its my birthday today.
And mom…
You just can't have good fun
When you're all dressed up
On a real nice day
Real nice clothes
And the sun's shining hot too.
And its your Birthday
Golly gee mom-
Its kinda hard to know
Just what to do

Here Again

We the flowers are
Here to say
I left you in the fall.
But now its spring
I'm here again
With all of
Life and beauty
To bring.
Hello - hello.

Nice

Blue sky
Clear sky
Sunny sky too
A real nice day
For you-and me too

Difficult Easy

The most difficult easy job-
There ever be, I think...
Is to care for-
Someone you know.
Everyday, that's'
What is known
As dai-ly
It wears you down
So quietly
You hardly know
But yet you do.
And others really, really
don't know.
But you-you really do.
Yet... this must be done
Cause its your shoulders
Its placed upon.
And creation helps
To get you thru.
The most difficult
Easy-job-there ever be...
One really, really, really-
Must do.

Water

Cold, cold water
And hot water too
Tastes really good
If its
Time for it to

A Butterfly

How can you
Catch a butterfly
When it goes
Flying by
Can you just
Point at it
With your finger-and say,
Please oh please
Stop here with me
While you fly by today.
Maybe its so hard
To catch a butterfly
-Just let them fly
They are so quiet
And so pretty
When they fly.

Away

When sickness-comes in
Rears its head
Making its scene-all around
All without a sound,
As quiet-as quiet can be
It seems to stay
Both night and day
So quiet it fights
Long-short its stay.
But when it leaves
It teaches well
That...
When sickness comes
Rears its head
Makes its scene all around
That...
When it comes
It likes to stay
And slowly, reluctantly leaves
Only when love
Creations love...
Drives it away.

A Crow

Today
A crow in a tree
Called down to me
"Caw caw caw"
I can talk
I can walk
I can fly
You can talk
You can walk
You cannot fly
And the crow flew away
Today.
That crow - that crow
But…
It was true
Tho.

Things

Reading, reading
I just like to read
And look at pictures too
Reading and pictures
And books are fun
And some
Really-really
Good things
To do.

Bubbles

Mix the water-soapy water
Make soap bubbles
Make them fly
In the wind, and faraway
Look, look, look,
At them go
Up, up, up, high
Small shiny bubbles
Way way high
In the blue, blue sky.

Again

When you're alone
In a house-and
You lay something down
It stays there-
Till you come back around
To pick it up-
And things kind of accumulate
Till you clean things up
To accommodate-clean again
Or the place begins too
Look like-well…
Lets don't go there,
Because we want clean air.
But when-
You're alone in a house
And, you lay something down it stays
Things accumulates like dirty souvenirs
Unless you accommodate, and-
straighten up things to be right, again.

Love

We speak of love
But what is love
Is it the same for you-for me?
Is it the same for me-for you?
This of course-we must think thru.
A mothers love, tho-
Is much the same
All life time thru
For the family, and children too, feel that-
The mother is there with love, to correct,
And to see them thru.
In what they do.
And a mothers love , is true
All the way
A life time thru
In what they do.
So a mothers love
Is really love, a lovely love.
For a mothers love
Never finishes-its never done.
Because a mother, children
Family too-if they to each
Are truly true…
They love, as one.

Something

Butterfly wings
don't make music-I can hear
But maybe butterflies
Sing songs other…
Butterflies can hear.
Music makes the quiet . Nice
And
The quiet makes music nice
Grasshoppers and crickets
Sing songs
When they like it, and sometime-
They sing all the day long.
The blue of the sky
Is where birds fly by.
And in the grass way…
Down low
Is where little mice go
Butterflies
Grasshoppers and crickets
Blue of sky
And everything
Has something to do
as each day passes thru

Nice

Butterflies flying
Real-real quiet
Flowers still
Green grass-on a hill
Children playing near
And…
Birds flying by
With a blue sky
Makes a nice day-in-a
Most beautiful way

Dance

Hula hoops
Of many colors
-Just as round
As they can be
Put them around
Your waist
Twist, twist, twist
Your body
Dance the hula
Dance the hula
One
Two
Three.

Sunshine

Today is a cloudy day
Today is a cloudy day.
Sunshine-sunshine
Bring back the sunshine.
A little girl said to me
She had it in her closet
don't know what we'll
Do without it.
Because…
Today is a cloudy day
Today is a real cloudy day.
Little girl...bring back the sunshine
We need the sunshine
Please-bring back the sunshine
Today.

Thank You

Blue, blue sky
I see you sky
Blue, blue sky
I like you sky.
Blue, blue sky
Will you stay
Blue, blue, pretty blue
All day sky.
And if you do
I will say,
Thank you, thank you,
All day
My way.

Flew

The bird flew
Up up
From the ground
Up up high in the tree
Moved all around
and flew-
Up, up,
Off in the sky
Off, off-
To far off and away
Like birds do,
All day

Cupcakes

Cupcakes round
And in a pan
Cupcakes eat
Them
With your hand
Cupcakes sweet
I like them too
And if you
Try them
So will you
Cause they're
Yummy

The Way

Bumps, bumps
Bumps
Little old bumps
In the road
Lead on to
Highways smooth
Like glass.
But we must pass thru
bumps, bumps
Little old bumps
In the highway
On the way.
All,
Must pass…
That way.

Folks

Think out of the box
Not as the ordinary-
They see the usual way,
Most everyday.
They're maybe-
Culture vultures and exist
In the box– all do the same
Everybody does a yes
Everybody does a no
When needed
To make and fix the mix
The status quo
Lets tour out of the box
Where the bad folks are where the good folks are
Where folks try and they cry
As rules there, they live by.
See the ghetto of
Both sides of the box where
The good the bad and the
Dreams are-folks live by.
Sometimes…
Think out of the box
Too.

A Kite

Oh, the tug
Of a kite
As it pulls on the string
As it flies
In the air.
Is a delight-
To a man-a boy
Or a girl
Or most anyone,
That hardly anything
Can compare.
As it flies-as it flies,
Gracefully-
In the air.

Things

Life consists
Of many things-
To get most good
That it can bring,
Consider the big
From many, many,…
Small of things.

Grass

The grass is green
Right over here
And I like green grass
Too.
It makes you feel
So very good.
And kind of tickles
Inside, all way thru.
Makes you think-
It thinks with you.

Passing Thru

The first time
Is hard to do
Just work real hard
and see it thru
The second time
will take some time
but will pass thru
Just give it time
The third time
will pass thru
like birds fly by
way up in blue.

Miraculous

Miracles we see them
Not in abundance
But they happen everyday
They come at times
They come in ways
Sometimes...
Not understood by those
That ask and need
Thru prayer and plead
But in ways that the creator
Who understands our needs
And answers in ways
understood in time
With time-our time
As given thru need-
Our need..
With miraculous love.
Miracles…
They happen everyday.

To Do

Puzzles and games
With crayons too
Clipboards books,
Paper, paste, pens-
And water paint
Too.
Makes a lot
Of good things
For children
To do.

Their Way

The boys are cooking today
They're mixing food
Their way.
There's corn here
Spoons over there
Cups here, dishes there
Water there and-
Here too.
-Just about everywhere
The stoves turned on
Faucets on
Cooks-good cooks
The boys are
Today they say the menu's
Hot lava.
Oh yes, the boys are cooking today
They're mixing
Food.
Their way.

Flying By

I saw an airplane
Flying by-right over
Where I seen-the moon
In the sky .
Not too high
-Just over the moon.
I seen it flying by
And the sun was shining
And the sky was blue.
And this airplane
-Just flew
And flew, and flew.

Confuses

Moonlight
Sunlight
Daylight too.
All at the
Same time
Confuses you.

Good

The littlest hotcake
Tastes so very, very good
It had all of
The scrapings
In the pan that was good
Left in the pan
Way, way down low
Scraped , scraped down and put in
The littlest hotcake-
That made it
So good.
So very good.

Everyday

From the rising sun
Each morning
Till each noon
Of everyday.
And the twilight
Then the evening
As it comes along the way.
There is a love
Deep in our hearts
For each and everyone
That is bright
As the rising sun
And as warm as
The sun at noon
Also lovely as the
Moon and stars at night
For each day we grow
Of this love we know
We feel-This love
We love-This love
For this love is …..True love
And true love-is beautiful.
Much like a rising sun…
At the beginning-
Of each morning

Wonderful Way

Some sleep by night
And play by day
Some sleep by day
And play by night
It's a wonderful way
To work and play
And play and work
And sleep that way.

A Speck

Billowing clouds-high-
In a clear-blue sky
Are beautiful-to the
Eye-to see
While
An airplane large high-high
In the sky-
Emerging from a vast billowing cloud
In the sky
Is hardly a speck in
The vast of sky.
An airplane large
Mid-the vast of sky
A speck– only a speck
why… why?
With
Billowing clouds
Thoughts...creation,
You and I.

Wet

The grass is wet
The slide is wet
The chairs are wet
The tables too
If we play outside
What will we do?
There is no sun today
But its not raining.
Mom told me-that-
Maybe everything is wet
From morning dew.
And maybe later
The sun will come out
then it will be
a nice day
And dry everything
I like it that way
don't you?

Paths

As we clean debris
From the paths
Of others
Also…
We must be aware
Of much debris
In the paths
Of our
own

Remember

Don't forget the past
Remember it too
Remember tho…
as you do-
The past…
has
Past thru

Butterflies

Oh look
There goes a butterfly
A little small
White butterfly
I see it flying by
Now look its friends
Are coming too
Two friends are with
The butterfly now.
1 butterfly
2 butterflies
3 butterflies
And they all fly away
That is what
Butterflies do all day.
Fly here
And there
And here
All day.

Around

Around the world
In many ways
We see things grow
We grow
In many ways
And day by day
Helped-hindered
Accepted-alienated
Loved-hated
Created
Desecrated
But help-in silence
Comes to choose (our choice)
Thru faith and use
Provided thru love
Our choice...
Never hidden
All around
All around-and,
The world...is
Really
Our choice
Of
The all around
Which makes
Each one's
World.

Ways

Feelings they make you feel
Then they're gone-and-
You don't feel none
Even the small ones
They make you feel good
they make you feel bad
Each as their way (silent way)
The big ones-the middle sized ones
They're about the same
Last longer tho
Some their memories
Never go
Feelings, guess you have them too
Mine maybe not as you
Yours-maybe not as me
Feelings really make you feel also... see
What life can be.
Feelings they make you feel
Then they're gone-and-
You don't feel none
Even sometime the small ones
Except... in silent ways
Thru... the days

Again

Love is as the rain
It comes again and again
No matter-whatever may be
Love is always there to see
It is as sunlight
From above-a cornerstone
A special home
Love is as the rain
It causes a strain
That remains-forever
And comes again and again
Is everlasting, abiding
And its eternal-ways
Comes…
Day after-loving days.

Rainbows

It rained today
Now
The sun is shining
The clouds are coming
Too
I like the rain
I like the sunshine
And clouds are-
Pretty too
I think…
Maybe today
I will go inside
And play
Maybe a rainbow
Will come today
I really like-
Looking at rainbows,
Too.

Today-Yesterday

What we see-and,
Think of today
Was seen and thought of
Yesterday and days gone by,
What will it be
For all to see
500 years from today
Including their
Yesterdays.
Just what do you-think
They will see
And what will it be

The Wind

Hey…
What color is the wind
Is it red, or green, or blue?
Why…
I really don't know
I never seen the wind
Have you?

Boxes

Cardboard boxes are, really neat
And most places
You can get em for free.
You can open them up
To go real, real wide
To make houses, and forts
To crawl inside.
Or make even an airplane
A sidewalk, truck, car or boat.
And my friend Michael…
Why he made-a submarine.
Then got inside,
Invited me in there too.
We just had lots, and lots,
And lots-I mean…
Just bunches, and bunches of fun.
Cardboard boxes are-
Really, really, neat-for almost-
Anything you could ever, ever,
Want to do
And my friends…
They like em too.

Puzzles

I like to do puzzles

They are really fun

And when you are thorough

Puzzles make you think

And have fun too.

Dripping

Dripping water
And falling rain
Are almost-
But not quite,
The same

Difficult Easy

The most difficult easy job-
There ever be, I think…
Is to care for-
Someone you know.
Everyday, that's,
What is known
As dai-ly
It wears you down
So quietly
You hardly know
But yet you do.
And other's really, really
Don't know.
But you-you really do.
Yet...This must be done
Cause its your shoulders
Its placed upon.
And creation helps
To get you thru.
The most difficult
Easy-Job-There ever be…
One really, really, really-
Must do.

Bicycle

I seen a boy-on a bicycle
I seen a girl-on a bicycle
I don't know where
They were going
They were moving very fast
And not so very slow.
But they were moving past
Now just where
Did they go?
I seen a boy-on a bicycle
I seen a girl-on a bicycle
They were going
They were going
Now they went.
And they are going
They are going
They are going they are going, going,
Gone.

Everywhere

Colors, colors, many colors
Reds, blues, yellows too
Purple, pink, black
Orange, green
White, brown.
Everywhere-there are
Many colors
All around-of Autumn leaves,
To be found.

Doves

I see-
Two doves in a tree
Looking down at me.
I see the doves
And the doves see me.
Happy are the doves
Happy as can be
Just…
Sitting and looking
In the tall, tall tree-
At, me.

Away

When sickness-comes in
Rears its head
Making its scene-all around
All without a sound,
As quiet-as quiet can be
It seems to stay
Both night and day
So quiet it fights
Long-short its stay
But when it leaves
It teaches well
That…
When sickness comes
Rears its head
It likes to stay
And slowly, reluctantly leaves
Only when love
Creations love…
Drives it away, creations-
Permanent, silent, special…way.

16

Very Interesting

A giraffes head-on the body
Of a horse.
Now that's a curious-
Fellow to see,
But I think I seen one.
And a cows head
With giraffes feet
Looked quite real
Also quite neat.
And there also was
An elephants head
On a cows torso
A very interesting
Girl or fellow.
Toys, toys
Animal toy's too-
Are fun…
When little boys-and little girls,
Make them,
For you.

Little Wagon

Little red wagon
With the little white wheels
Rolling up-
And down the hill
Filled with boys and girls
Toys-
Dolls, teddy bears
Sometime-
Empty too.
Little red wagon
We all-
Really, really
Like you,
Love you-
Too.

A Kite

Little boy-little girl
Running
With that kite
On a string
Flying seems a fun
Thing to do.
And a something
For you remember
Too.

A Mistake

One little mistake
That's all it took
Should everything and all
Be overlooked.
For the good in something,
Maybe…
from one little mistake
Might be all-
That it takes
For a good look…
to be took
Helping-everything.

I See

Two butterflies
Flying round and round
Two butterflies I see.
Two butterflies
Making not a sound
Flying round and round.
Two white butterflies-
Flying round me.

For You

Don't pull up the bridge
Behind you
Build on it– don't just sit
Don't pull up the bridge
Make it more solid
Ridged, ridged-do that to it
That's what's needed
Don't pull up the bridge
Its really needed now
Find a way to cross it somehow.
Behind you-never ever
Pull up the bridge
Your rainbow-your goal
Is on the other side
Waiting-over the bridge-waiting for you.

Different

Gosh its hard-to run a house
On your own
There's so much to do
When you're all alone
You have to cook
Clean the house
go to the store
And much more
Even go to bed,
Pace yourself-
Get up when it's right
But…
There's some things
You can still
Think and do on your own
And that's tie your shoes
All alone,
While It's still…and they wait
Quite different
To run a house on
Your own.
At least right at first.

Hey…

I got a snail
And you don't
Have one.
I got a snail
Bet-cha wish you
Had one
You can't have
The snail
I got
Cause I got the snail
And you-do not
HA-HA

Inward

Happiness is wonderful
Inward joy is beautiful
Happiness can go away
Inward joy-if true-
Is there everyday,
For you

Nice

A little house-not too big
Not too small
With rooms and all
Dolls-toys-chairs-beds-
Dressers too.
Where my friends and I
Can play anytime,
Even all day, if we want to.
I would like that
It would be nice.
A little house-like maybe a dollhouse
Not too big
Not too small very strong
With rooms, toys, chairs, beds
Dressers too
And all, it would be very nice
Everyday-we could play and play and play.
Then, take with us– where…
We go– everyday.
That would be nice-
Very nice.

A Port

All alone, all alone
All alone-
On a timeless sea
Drifting, drifting,
Drifting on
With none near,
Close by me.
Others far, far away
Near the world's-deep curve-
And them..
Very soon, I won't see.
All alone, all alone, all alone
In a boat-on a timeless sea,
Drifting, drifting
Drifting on.
To a port-
Not now known
To me.

Help

Please help me
Thru-my way.
Not your way.
Try to see my way.
For your way
Confuses me…
Now

Someway

Remember everybody
Someway
Because everybody
Likes to be
Remembered
Somehow
A good way
Everyday

Maybe

Don't hit-don't hit
Use your words,
Can't you see
There's nothing here
Except little old me.
I have nothing to fight with
Or don't you see.
Maybe you do-
Maybe something's here
You want.
And maybe that's why
You're hitting
Little old me.
But use your words
Please…
I'm sure we can talk-
Don't hit-don't hit
Thank you.

This Way

The world is beautiful
And full of loveliness
Is the world more
Beautiful because
I came this way
Or will it be-
More beautiful
When I have gone
Away.
I think sometime
Sometime I think
This way.
And then I try to make the best I can-
Of everyday
To make…
The world a better
Place-because…
I came this way.

Where

Children-children
Where are your shoes
We can't find them
What can we do?
Go play, play, play
Play, play, play
Play in the sandbox
Till you do.

You

I don't want what
You got anymore
Cause you ain't the same
As you was before
You see things in a
Different way than
You seen the same thing before
Hey you ain't the same person
Now that I seen before.
What you talk
Ain't the same talk
You talked before
You say things now
You ain't never said before
They ain't from my point of view
Don't know where they came from
They sure ain't sweet sweet peaches
They be real, real, sour plums
When you walk
You don't walk
Like you did before
You be shakin flab like jello
In a great big vat
Shakin old-jiggly, jiggly, jiggling-kinda fat
I don't want you anymore
You ain't the same
As you was before
You gotta change
We gotta change
For me to want you
As before.

Wonder

Parasols-
Are good
For rain and
Good for sunshine
Too.
I wonder-
Just how many
Real good things
That parasols
Can do?
There must be more
I'm really sure-
I wish that we
But knew.

Snail

She has a snail
On her finger
She is carrying it around
And the snail
Does not even make-
A sound.
Maybe the snail wonders-
What she will do,
With the snail
On her finger
When she is thru.
What do you think
She will do?

Friends

Friends are nice
When we talk
When we sing
When we play
When we color books together
We are friends
Friends are nice
And when we play
In the sand
Or we climb in the trees
Or we play in the pool
Or you play where you please
And we talk
And we play together.
We are friends-
Friends are nice.

Shine

Glitter, glitter
Stars they glitter-
Twinkle
And they shine.
Way up in
The night time sky
Just about-
All the time

Little Ant

Hey little ant climbing
Up the apple tree,
Making friends
With the others
Living on the tree.
Are you going all way
To the top
Where sunshine is
Bright as it can be?

To Winter

I really liked that green skirt
You wore-with the
Black flowers and embroidery
I remember flowing,
Woven in the scene
As you walked-
It seemed and did
Create a peaceful
Just lovely something
To the day...your way
With,
That green and black skirt
On.
You brought sunshine..
Like spring blossoms
Though winter-
That day.

The Complaining Witch

My beds too hard
My beds too soft
My chocolates too hot
My chocolates too cold
My feets cold
My hands are cold
My rooms too hot
My rooms too cold
The windows open too wide
Open the window
The lights too bright
The lights too dim
What's the matter with
You folks?
If you don't listen to me soon-
I'll just get on my broom
And fly to the moon
Turn it around
To be dark in your rooms
Then you'll see-
Hee-hee-hee,
Hee, hee, hee, hee, hee, hee, hee, hee

Fun Things

Wagons with children
And toys and things
   go fun places.
And do fun things.

Together

Maybe-
Just spending time together
Visiting family
And friends
Going places together
At Christmas,
Or Holiday times.
Instead of so much
Exhaustion and
Excessive spending-sometime,
At Holiday time.
Might be-nice to do
Maybe-huh, might be nice.
Lets try it.

A Tree

Blossoms, leaves,
On the limb of a tree
In spring time and summer
Gives apples for you…
And apples for me.
Then during autumn's song
When shadows grow long
And leaves fall down.
Apples remind us
All year long
That a blossom a leaf
On the limb of a tree
Left apples for you-
And apples for me.

A Million Times

Surprise surprise
No peekin with your eyes
Betcha can't guess
What I'm holding in my hands.
Now you can peek
If yuh really want to.
Aw, its just a lady bug
And an old creepy crawlie-
Not a super big surprise
Like I wanted it to be.
Yeah, but if you tried
Really really.
Maybe a million times hard,
It could be.

Wagon

I like it
I like it
I want it too.
My wagon-my wagon
My little red wagon
And little red wagon-
I like you so…
I'll take you
I'll take you
Anywhere-I go.

Early

In early morning
When its raining
Soft…
Just falling down
That's usually
An unexpected
Nice understood
Special-
Kind of sound
Secretly, desired.
Mid sleep…
In the early morning.

Thread

Hold on by a thread
Don't turn it all loose
Look-look…
There's the sun
There's the dawn
Hold on-move along
I see a path way
For a new way
A new day
Don't turn it all loose
Hold on by the thread
Weave it-weave…
And use it-in,
The new song
As you move along

Mystery

From a tiny seed
Some mustard grew
From a tiny seed-sunflowers grew
From a cloudy sky
A large storm grew.
From a heavenly glow
A rainbow grew.
Then all around
Seemed beautiful-signaling
To all…
Perhaps less pressure
From the storm-would be
All a mystery
Like life in seed
Clouds bringing storms
Sustaining water
Beautiful healing, rainbows-come and,
In a way
That's accepted, rejected
And lovely
Thru creation
To all-for all.

Difficult

To release, the wind
To never return
Would be difficult
To release what one
Has built with love
Thru a lifetime
Is much the same
To release a love
To never return
Is much the same
To then relize a memory
That was built
Then has a name
Is beautifully lovely
But…
To release the wind
To never return tho
Is difficult.

From Far – Away

Its sure getting late
My wife's not feeling good
And she is 88
At first that was-
Harder to understand
But now its understood.
I'm old myself - soon be 81
Course-age is just a number. Leaving
Much to be done.
Would like to talk to others my age
But most have left the stage I'm on-
Gone other places-I guess better
Don't even correspond
Not even with a letter.
So I most talk to someone far-way
We talk and laugh about everyday.
Gosh, it's sure, getting late tho-
Wife's not feeling good -and she is 88
But you know…the someone
I think I'll talk with-
From far-away
Seems to brighten up, most everyone's-
Everyday, sure does mine.
With just plain, old fashioned
Love, from far-away
Know what he sure is kind

Children

You are trusted by a child
Once you have
Earned their
Respect,
And once-you have earned it,
Children never forget it.

Of Blue

Oh look and see
Oh look and see
The sky of blue
I see.
There is no cloud
In the sky I see
Only sky of blue
Over you and me.

Mothers

Mothers teach the first things
Much as God would do.
When with and…
Thru the all of this
While growing more
Each day
The teaching of a mother
Is I love you more
Each day.

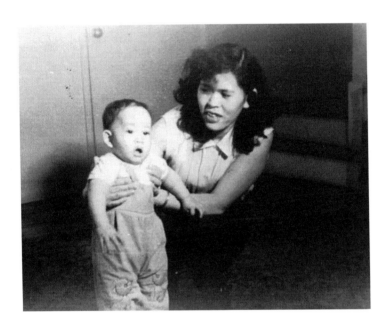

A Butterfly

If you could-ride a butterfly
And fly thru the trees
Of a forest
Deep and green.
Over hills-over valleys
Even, oceans
Quite unseen
Wouldn't that be fun
To do.
Very quiet-
And not tell-anyone.

Rain Rainbows

The rain came down
But not too hard
Where children played
Out in the yard.
Then sunshine came,
And with the rain…
Made a beautiful
Rainbow,
Children just love-
In the sky-the rainbow.
With everything
Damp
After the rain
After the rain
Came down.

26

Golly Gee

Red ball-red ball
Big ball-small ball
Red ball-red ball
Bounce for me.
Red ball small ball
Big ball red ball
Red ball red ball
Roll for me.
Roll ball red ball
Big ball small ball
Bounce ball big ball
Fly for me.
Big ball small balls
Roll balls bounce balls
Red balls red balls
Golly gee.

Mysterious

Of the sunshine
Of the rain
Of the clouds
The thunder too-
Of the blossom-flowers
A small humming bird
This-too
And even expressions
On a face-of-
Young-old-
A rising moon
A full moon
Mysterious lightening too.
But especially
All this-
And most of all.
Our mother
And gods love.
Making all things possible

_____

For everything
Thru-the sounds of love, eternal
Quite different to all
Everyday
In special ways...is lovely, beautiful too,
All the way thru.

Crows

3 crows in a row
Flying slow
Now where did
Those 3 crows go
Oh I see them
Over there in a tree
Those 3 crows
Are watching me.

27

Up High

Oh say little cloud, little cloud
Way, way up high
In the sky so blue.
And in the quiet too
"Hello"
Where are you drifting too?
Little cloud-little cloud
So high, in the bright blue
Morning sky.

To See

Lily's my doll
And goes with me
To see the things
I love to see
Like lady bugs-with spotted wings
Or jungle gyms where pipes and bars
And shaky bridges are.
Then while she rests-
Just looking at, nice blue up in the sky
We think about rabbits
That whisper quiet…
Something like-a butterfly,
Passing by.
Lily's my doll-and goes with me
And see the things...I love to see-
We are friends

Maybe

Did you see that
It was really big?
Yes I seen it
It was not too big,
To me it was more small.
Then maybe we're-
Not seeing what
We see-or think we see
At all.
But did you see that?
It was big
Real big...maybe.

Sunshine Sunshine

Sunshine hot
Or sunshine cold
When you're angry
I am told.
You can't think right
And won't do right.
So you should do
As you were told.

I'm Angry

I'm angry, angry, angry
From my head, right to my toes.
I would get lots more angry
But that's all of me
As you can see.
And
"I'm"
Angry, angry
"Angry!"
I think…
As I can be

At Times

At times
What you do
Is confusing to me
At times
What I do
Is confusing to you
May be its better
That way
Because it makes
What we think to be true
Come thru-better
As true-that way

I Can

I'm only three
And I would
If I could
Awe I think, I can
But right now
To ride a unicycle
Is kind of hard for me.
A bicycle with
Wheels of two
I can almost do.
But with training wheels
I can ride it too.
And a tricycle
With 3 wheels-if its not too very big.
I can ride-
Any old time.

Not Easy

Numbers are not easy to learn
They really make you kind of squirm
The one is easy
And 2-3-4
They make you think
Just more and more.
But 4-5-6 are not so hard
And 6-7-8 I think are great
9 and 6 look the same to me
And at 10 you start to write
Then everything starts all
Over again.
Numbers are not easy to learn
They make you kind of squirm.

Snail

She has a snail
On her finger
She is carrying it around
And the snail
Does not even make-
A sound.
Maybe the snail wonders-
What she will do,
With the snail
On her finger
When she is thru.
What do you think
She will do?

To Watch

I like to watch
The humming birds
Just sit and fly away.
They fly so very fast-
They fly so very slow-
They fly and stop
Right in the air,
Wings all a-flutter there.
With their feathers-
Oh so pretty-
When the sun shines on them too,
Kind of green and many
Colors-and sometime
Even blue.
I like to watch the humming
Birds-most folks they really do.

Small

Tiny-as small
As it can be
With babies as small
As a little bee.
The humming bird
Can hover-and fly
In the air.
As fast as it
Wants to,
And go just where
It wants.
Almost anytime,
Anywhere.

Heavenly Beauty

Heavenly beauty
Lies in all
Creation offers
For all is good
If understood
That creations way…
Is very good.

Sunshine

You light up my life
A special way
Like sunshine does
When it shines
Each day.
Then the days
They fly
Good thoughts
Pass by
When I think of you
Or I even try
You light my life-
You light up my life
A special way
Everyday– everyday
Every…
Single day.

Two Birds

Two birds in a tree
My friends see them too
Two birds in a tree
Now what will they do?
Will they just sit
In a tree,
That's a nice place to be
Or will their friends
Come by
And they all fly away
Two birds in a tree
Two birds that we see
Now what do you think
Those two birds
Will do?

Look

Oh look mommie look
At the clouds I see
I see-
A horse, a dog
And a sheep or two,
Crawling by, "look, look" -
Can't you see them
In the sky
Going by.
Oh yes, I don't need to look
Child, I seen them before
Now-I see only clouds, clouds, clouds
Everyday
In the sky, passing by.

For You

Close the door
And lock the door
Then close the windows too
Check the house
All thru the house
Then you can sleep-
The house is safe,
For you-me too.

Every Day

From the rising sun
Each morning
Till each noon
Of everyday.
And the twilight
Then the evening
As it comes along the way.
There is a love
Deep in our hearts
For each and everyone
That is bright
As the rising sun
And as warm as
The sun at noon.
Also lovely as the
Moon and stars at night.
For each day we grow
Of this love we know
We feel-this love
We love-this love
For this love is...true love
And true love-is beautiful.
Much like a rising sun...
At the beginning-
Of each morning.

Bye Bye

A shadow passed me
On the ground
A bird was flying by
The bird flew high
Way in the sky
The shadow went-with the bird,
Bye bye.

Of Lovely

Think of the blossom
The flowers too.
Think of a seed-
A sapling-a small-and...
Large tree too.
Think of an egg,
Small, medium-large bird too.
Think of a cloud, a storm-
A rainbow too.
Think of dawn, sunlight
Happiness, a beautiful day too.
Think of noon, twilight
Evening, moonlight, stars-
Just shining thru.
Think of all this...
With family, flowers
Sunshine, storms
Rainbows, twilight, evenings.
Aged with love-
And...
Of lovely memories,
Too.

Clocks

Tick, tock, tick tock
Clocks they have a way
Thru their tick tock
Tick tock, tick tock
They tell seconds
Minutes, hours of each day
Thru their tick tock
Tick tock, tick tock
We can count the days, weeks
Months, years away
All lifetimes thru
Their lifetime too
Those clock they
Tick tock, tick tock
That's what they do
And when they're thru
Other clocks they
Tick tock, tick tock
Too
Clocks have a way
They certainly do
They
Tick tock, tick tock
Lifetimes thru
Tick tock, tick tock
Nights and days
Tick tock, tick tock
All
The way.

Calendars

I really do like calendars
I like em all over the place
Hang one over here
Hang one over there
To look at and see
Wherever you be
Sometime days get mixed
That's all right, with me too
Whatever day you think
Its all right with you
I really do like calendars
I like em all over the place
Calendars make you and time…
Really-top ace. I -
Like, I really like,
Calendars.

Thankful

Count the many blessings
Given freely
To be thankful for
And…
If you're honest
You'll find more
From the Creator
To be
Thankful
Than unthankful
For.

33

Look

Oh look mommie look
At the clouds I see
I see-
A horse, a dog
An a sheep or two
Crawling by, "look, look" -
Can't you see them
In the sky
Going by.
Oh yes, I don't need to look
Child, I seen them before
Now-I see only clouds, clouds, clouds
Everyday
In the sky, passing by.

Real Cold

Cold water, cold water
Real cold-cold water
Is where
Fish, whales, octopus too
Live, play, sleep there too.
Because that's their home
And they have to.
But folks like you
And me-
Touch real cold cold water
Only if…
We really, really
Have to.

My Friend

At my friends little house
That I see-
Way over there.
Maybe his mom will have,
Something nice for my friend
And me.
Like cookies and milk-or-
Maybe ice cream too.
Or maybe hot cakes
And chocolate syrup.
When we are thru
At my friends little house
When I visit with my friend
Over there.

Please Sit

Humming bird
In a tree-looking down
I think-at me
Humming please sit and stare
I like to see you-
Sitting there,

Believe

What one believes
Is what's conceived
In the mind to believe
Facts of true
Maybe turned
As some do-to
Make way for a
More lovely day
To conceive what
One wants to believe.
-But I believe
In-Spring
Summer-
Autumn-winter
Too.
As the seasons
Bring just lovely
Thru.

Someone

Lonesome-lonesome
You can be-
When someone's not near
You can see.
That's not been near
For many days.
Or, that's been near
But not real near
In thought or other
Ways.
Lonesome can touch
In silence or...
Thru feeling's that
Are deep-real deep
as oceans are.
Or stars in heaven's
High
Lonesome, lonesome
You can be
When someone's-not near
To touch -to love-sincere.
You can see.

Most Beautiful

Sunshine-blue skies
White drifting clouds too.
I can see a most
Beautiful day
don't you too.

Imagine

Other planets
Are so far away
And sometime
Seem so near
They look like
Bright lights
In the sky
Or sometime
Like an
Airplane passing
By.
Or things we can
Imagine
Way-high
Up, in the sky

Leaves

One leaf fell down
I seen if flutter
Thru the window
It fell soft-silent
To the ground
And it fell in-
Such a way
I thought about it
All thru the day.
I guess leaves fall
Silent…
Some where-every where
Seen thru windows,
Or some way-
Making feelings…
Every day.

Independence Day

A day to remember
A day to reflect
On much of the past
The present too
Of much of the all
Memories may pull us thru.
As we accept-reflect
Then bring to today a wonder full acceptable
Independence day
A day to remember
Happy independence day

My Shadow

Hey - "hey you"… don't step on my shadow
I'll move it away
I don't want anybody
I mean anybody
To step on my shadow.
I made it-I made it
It's mine all mine
Don't step on my shadow
You hear me
Do you hear me…
Don't step on my shadow
Its mine.

Asking

Thanks for liking… asking…
How are you?
That to me-means-
You in some way know…
For you've been there too,
And know-
Also can understand
What I'm now going thru.
Thanks for liking-asking.
And…
Thanks again
Those words,
Had a golden touch-
They meant…
much
Much.

Me

I'm an individual-
Can't you see that's me
I may be mixed
With this and that
but can't you see-that's me
A little bit
From this country-and some..
From that country-tho,
The minority-that's what you see.
But inside me…
I'm not a loser
Tho you may think, I am
I'm a separate individual
Can't you see-
That's me.

Difficult

To release, the wind
To never return
Would be difficult
To release what one
Has built with love
Thru a life time
Is much the same
To release a love
To never return
Is much the same
To then realize a memory
That was built
Then has a name
Is beautifully lovely
And…
To release the wind
To never return tho-
Is difficult.

Little

I seen a little humming bird
Sitting in a tree
And the little humming bird
Was quiet-just as quiet
As can be.
Sometime the little humming bird
I think was watching me
Sometime the little humming bird
Was looking far away,
I seen a little humming bird
A little tiny humming bird today.

In Day

Seagull with your coat of white
Do you ever fly at night?
Or do you only
Fly in day.
To have sunshine,
Light your way.

Shaded

Dark and halfway shaded
Neath blue of sky
With drifting clouds
Of grayish white.
Quite distant-nearby,
with
Hills of green-
A lovely Salinas,
Early March scene
Of, wintery California
I see….
Neath blue of sky
With drifting clouds-
Today

Why

Isn't it a shame
There could have-
Been more done
But wasn't
I wonder why
Maybe didn't try
Perhaps that was why
If a try had been made
Maybe things would
Be better
If a try had been made
Maybe things
Would be worse
Or maybe-even the same
Isn't it a shame
So little was done
Why if we would-
Have tried just a little more
Cause no one else did
We...could have won

On Board

The ship of intelligence
Is sailing thru
Now what are you
Going to do?
Will you get on-
There's room, lots of room
On the ship for you.
You may have to change
Your way of thinking.
To keep your boat, from sinking.
Because the ship of intelligence
Is here to stay.
And all that desire
Can get on today
Come on, come on-
Get on board, get on board
Today.

Hope

Change, change, change
To the change that change
Can bring
Bring, bring, bring
The change-we hope
That it can do.
To bring change.

Preventing

Sometime in a storm
The wind hits full force
Nearly blows us away.
Sometime in a storm
The wind's full force
First strikes a wall
We are spared the winds
Forceful strike in that way.
Sometimes patience as wind
Slows anger…
As the wind and a wall-
Preventing,
Mistakes or the greatest
Of falls.

Be Happy

If she's happy
Then I'm happy
And if-I'm happy
I feel, the whole worlds
Happy.
And its nice
To be happy
Isn't it…
Please just-
Be happy
Today...

The Spirit

As the wind-the spirit came
Not heard-not seen
But understood
In a way that enlightened
The day
And revealed love
Silently-beautifully
Felt, seen, for each-
Quite differently.
Yes, the spirit came-as the wind
As a breath-healing, caring
Giving life, thru love.

Passing

Tearing, ripping, breaking, smashing
The earth quake
Comes thru
Quickly-then,
Goes on its way.
Only to speak…
Demandingly
Attentively
Individually
Thunderously
Mysteriously
Warning...to never forget,
Creations powers - as you pass
Closely, together
Passing thru.

Many Doors

Thru the open doors
Come many
From all cultures and beliefs-for
Reasons unknown
With stories to tell
Understood by others
At times when the doors
Open to all are
Used by those of
Choice thru seasons
Spring, summer, fall
Winter with its snows
Covering the good, bad.
Happy are the many
That enter-leave
Stay continually passing
Thru the open ever existing of…
Doors so lovely,
The many always open doors
Where teaching
Of the creators
love-can always
Be found.

Lengthy

A connection with
Strength as the dark night
Tested by starlight bright
Exists thru centuries
Of lengthy age
Very like a bond of
Mother daughter
Father son
The dark the light-for-
All have a connection
A bond unseen
That remains forever
A bond a connection
And a bond of
Everlasting love.

Birds

As birds soar
On high
The world
Watches
Them fly.

Far-Away

In the far Eastern areas
In the land of faraway
I purchased me a bicycle
To cruise streets
Of the faraway
On the streets of
Faces many.
I seen friend and foes
There too
And I seen faces
Of fair and fairer
Of women many and fewer few
Shops also many-in a land faraway.

Traveling On

Two wheels has a bicycle
As they cycle-round and round
Taking one down the road and along
Two wheels has a motorcycle
As they cycle round and round
Taking one down the road-cycling round.
And the airplane-and the train
And the ship-the submarine
Birds-butterflies
Sun, moon, and yes-the stars
Flowers, trees, grass-people too
Seems everything cycle, cycles
round and round-starts go back
Their special way
As they go
With years-with days
Traveling, moving
Traveling on.

A Slide

Climb to the top
And zip you're down.
A ride on a slide
Is climb up-
And slide down.

Jungle Gyms

Slides-stairs
Walking places too.
There's just lots of things
On a jungle gym
For everyone-
To do.

Something

There's a something
In the atmosphere
That fills December days
A feel a glow
That inside kind of
Changes folk'ses ways.
Perhaps...its
The crisp of air
The neon lights
With children...tinsel everywhere.
Small bells that chime
To bring the time
Of Christmas
Closely near.
And birth a special day
Just filled with love
That fills
The atmosphere
Of wishing-everyone
Just everywhere…
A very
Merry Christmas
And, a…
Lovely-Happy New Year.

Eternally

There is no face in dark
But only dark to see
There is no light in dark
In dark-there's mystery
Mysterious hides,
There in the dark.
The face of light is there
To see
On all around in all
There's mystery
There's also love that one
Can find-for each
In individual ways
That folds-unfolds
With flowing days.
Yet dark and light
Are in love too
They blend as one
To teach and guide
Give day and night,
With lovely light
In moderation
Eternally…
Light day and night
Carefully..
Flowing-
with– creation.
For…
There is no face in dark
Only dark to see.

Our Own Way

Cultures differ in the way
We greet each other
Things we say
Making beautiful
In the way-we do…
Much the same things,
Our own way.

Mornings

Today mornings late… Does it ever
Seem like that
To you?
Sometime…
Yes of course
It seems like
That to me,
Golly-ghee.
Mornings come strange
At times.

The Rim

Along the rim-of the ocean
Way off
Where clouds seem to-gather here
Sometime there
And soothes to the oceans roll
With a Love that's forever true.
Along the rim of the ocean
Something waits silent
Rolling, rolling soothing thru
To those who listen-
Like me, like you
Watching…
Where the sky-
Meets the sea.

Very Wonderful

Natures very wonderful
And fills us up
Until we're full with youth
And then we're gifted with-
The gift of age.
Which is for each an art
Right from the very start.
And continues on and on
Right to the very end,
Yes natures very wonderful
Fills us up until we're full
With gifts of youth and age
Then lets us develop each…
Page, by page, by page
And then with age
Nature closes
Up-the door
Takes the light away
And doesn't give us…that
Special light anymore.

The Same

To live a long life
With illness there too
Perhaps not the same
As a life not so long
With no illness
Oh life has a way
It teaches each day
Whether illness or not
And this lesson
Is equal to all
And not soon forgot.

Someway

Remember, Oh remember
To remember.
Because everybody likes-
To be remembered.
Some way,
A good way, someway,
everyday

Always There

Of our growing together where flowers grow free
And Night Hawks soared summer skies
Whip-poor-wills spoke soothingly too
Summery evenings thru.
Where school buses-of red, white and blue
Served in home many ways
And children-families, parents grew.
Marriage too,
Thru sacred given days-was marvelous.
Also along life's road sceneries beautiful grew
There thorns-there blossoms
Beautiful flowers thrived.
We picked, we chose, we planted seeds
Then gathered harvest of our choosing.
And along the way-where we strolled
Love was always there
In all the seasons air-growing
Bonding together
Silently, lovingly, spiritually, eternally,
Of my then-leaving...quietly
All that's grown together
Along life's road
Thru memories-amazing...thru faith
And in a way-as beautiful-
Like each sunrise, sunset, soft evening
Each given day
In Love-with Love.
Please understand-Lovingly
And…
Forever-our true love was there.

When

When you and yer mate
Are old and one gets sick-
And find yer, all alone.
Why ya, really then can quick
Find out who yer friends,
They really be..
For most they seem
To scatter just like buckshot-
Or maybe, clouds in the sky
And wave maybe once or twice
As they meander-passing by.
Then others maybe-they don't even try.
And...Some you don't even think about-
They really do come by.
When yer old-with yer mate
And one gets sick.
A whole lot passes by.
In just the blink-of an eye.
And friends are beautiful-
Why, they're like…
Sunshine in the sky.

Shoe

My shoe - My shoe
I can't find my shoe
Where in the world is my shoe?
Say say-look at the moon
Look at the moon
May be the man in the moon has your shoe.

You And Me

Psst hey-
Do you know where
They came from?
They're not one of us
Yes I do-why all the fuss.
Do you want all the flowers
To be the same?
All folks to have the same name.
Everybody to look, think the same
What kind of place-would that be
Yes I see they're not like us-
And that don't matter to me
So don't make a fuss
Its better for us-
To see different-be different
And then in good agree
It makes a better
Both you-and me.

Work

All must work
For work is good
It makes one understood
Appreciated-for what they do
Very understood
In each his way-
For work
Gives sense
In eternal ways
Beautiful
Work must be
For all to see
And be shared
Equally.
All must work

Speak

Rocks speak-
With silence
To the listening ear
From inside-out
Year after year
After year
After year
Heard with fabulous beauty
By the right listening ear
Year after year
After year
After year
In lovely ways
Creating
Lovely days– in,
Natural ways.

Oop's

Wash the clothes
Fold the clothes
Put the clothes away
Ooop's one stockings missing
What can we do?
Find the stockings
Put it away.
Then we can be thru.

Mystery

From a tiny seed
Some mustard grew
From a tiny seed-sunflowers grew
From a cloudy sky
A large storm grew.
From a heavenly glow
A rainbow grew.
Then all around
Seemed beautiful-signaling
To all…
Perhaps less pressure
From the storm-would be
All a mystery
Like life in seed
Clouds bringing storms
Sustaining water
Beautiful healing, rainbows-come and,
In a way
That's accepted, rejected
And lovely
Thru creation
To all-for all.

Here

Hey-you're close
You're so near
I didn't know-that you
Were here.
You came in, real soft.
Now we must do
What we must do
Quick…
So you can be,
Aloft,
On your way.
And others-
Won't know,
You came by here…
Today.
(till they look)

From Far – Away

Its sure getting late
My wife's not feeling good
And she is 88
At first that was-
Harder to understand
But now its understood.
I'm old myself - soon be 81
Course-age is just a number. Leaving
Much to be done.
Would like to talk to others my age
But most have left the stage I'm on-
Gone other places-I guess better
Don't even correspond
Not even with a letter.
So I most talk to someone far-way
We talk and laugh about everyday.
Gosh, it's sure, getting late tho-
Wife's not feeling good -and she is 88
But you know…the someone
I think I'll talk with-
From far-away
Seems to brighten up, most everyone's-
Everyday, sure does mine.
With just plain, old fashioned
Love, from far-away
Know what he sure is kind

Deep

Tho the winds may blow
And the rains comes down
And the snows fall heavy
Just swirling round
The great storm sometime
Comes from within
Deep deep in the heart
Where few are let in
Unlike the wind
The rains-the snow
That all know.

Quiet

Early in the morning
When its dark outside
And even the lights that shine
Seem, quiet too.
There's not much to do.
So-I'm quiet too.

Your Needs

Little bird up in the sky
You find your needs
While yet you fly.
You do not store
In barns below
For as you seek-
Each day by day
Your needs are there
Each-every day.
Little bird up in the sky
You find your needs
Where 'ere you fly.
Given with love-from love
And-just for you,
As you pass swiftly, softly,
Lovely, thru.

Morning

When its 3 o' clock
In the morning
and its cold and dark outside
When it's raining
outside too
I can hear rain
Soft falling down,
And it's 3 o' clock
In the morning
It seems best-if-
I go back to sleep
Not get up…
Move around,
Because its really, really,
Nice to sleep
When the rain-
Is falling down.

On Water

The light of
The full moon on high-
On water,
To the eye.
Is just
Fantastically
Beautiful…
To the roving eye.

Seems Like

Sometimes
When you do-a lot of things
It seems like
You didn't do anything
And sometimes
When you-don't do
Anything
It seems like
You never get thru.

Ran

The little boy ran
The little girl ran
They ran, and ran, and ran
As fast as they could go
Just why they ran
So really fast
Maybe they only know
But they ran-they run
They run they run
Because I seen them go

Confusion

Clean your room
Clean your room
Sweep your area-with a broom.
To have brooms and not use them
Makes utter confusion.
To have windows and doors
That lead to sunlight
And yet remain in the dark
And leave all that's done
As only half.
Clean the all-
And make a path
Then…
Clean your room
Clean your room
Sweep your area
With a broom-Clean...

An Afternoon

Eating fried chicken
On Sunday afternoon
Watching the cars go by
Eating fried chicken-
My wife and I
Under a blue, hazy sky.
Enjoying the world
In a beautiful way
This lazy, hazy day.
Eating fried chicken
At a restaurant on a slow moving day
Having a marvelous time
Freely passing…
A lovely, simply lovely,
Afternoon-
Away.

Sunflower

Look look
I just seen
A big yellow sunflower
With leaves of green
Maybe that sunflower
With green leaves
I just seen.
Will have seeds
Sunflower seeds.
I really, really-do…
Just like-
Sunflower seeds.

A Beautiful Way

Sunshine-blue skies
Green grass-flowers
A rainbow
And sunshine high
In a blue blue sky
Makes a beautiful day
In a most-
Lovely way.

Around

Around the world
In many ways
We see things grow
We grow
In many ways
And day by day
Helped-hindered
Accepted-alienated
Loved-hated
Created
Desecrated
But help in silence
Comes to choose (our choice)
Thru faith and use
Provided thru love
Our choice…
Never hidden
All around-and
The world...is,wholly offered.

Independence

The green of the grass
A sky crystal blue
A bird soaring high
The morning quite new
Twilight then evening
A night with dark too
The moon fully bright
And stars showing centuries light
Each with an independence
All its own
Yet dependent on its
Independence as the green
Of the grass to live and
Be each its own.
Is nature, is lovely, is beautiful.

In January

A Bumble Bee in January
This spectacle-This…I did see.
And it-came in the garage
With me
Between the hour of two
And just before the hour of two
And before the hour of three.
He flew round, and round,
And round-noisily-
As if searching, that,
Did he.
I don't know what was in
The garage
In January…
For the Bumble Bee to see.
He stayed only for a-
Little while
Then flew out and on his way.
Quite strange, quite strange
Quite strange, quite strange
Quite strange– this I must say.
But I wonder why in January
When its cool here-
Very cool here, now.
Just why,
Did a Bumble Bee-
Come here, when I was near
To fly in my garage
While I was here.
To somehow visit with me
Today.
And then went on its way.
A Bumble Bee in January.
Then-maybe…
Perhaps twas a nice
New years present for me
And the January Bumble Bee
In its buzzing, droning way,
Wearing its very black jacket
(and that) all the visit thru.
Still quite strange-
Quite strange-quite strange
Quite strange to me.
A January Bumble Bee.
Between the hour of two-
And before, the hour of three.
Visiting-me

Those

Why do you talk
With those
Who've left and gone.
Do you think you're here and all alone.
We
We're here and keep
You company
We hear you speak
And call to them.
Perhaps them you see
Where 'ere
They be
And keep you company.
When to them you
Speak in a way
You understand
And you command
Perhaps your way
From day to day.
But…
Why do you talk
To those who've
Left here
You're not alone.
Is it for need
You want them near
Or do you..they hear?
Do you...they hear?
Do you...see them
Do they...see you
We'd like to know,
Some day, some way.

Really

The wind…
We never see
But only feel
And see-where it could possibly-have been.
Aren't they…
Eternally amazing
The wind and love.
Yet, the two of them
We… never really
See.

Travel

To the rainbows edge
That's where I'd go
I love to travel far
I love to look up
In the sky
And watch the far
Off stars.
And feel just wind
Blow in my face
While trees bend low
As they embrace
As distant winds
Blow grass down low
And birds just frolic high
While clouds drift
In an open far-off sky
Oh that rainbows edge
It calls real soft
And beckons-relentlessly
At times
Of fortune, to-adventure yes
It has just for me-reserved,
That's golden yes sublime.
But to get away
And let just adventure
Have its way
This time-it must wait
Its just too late
For I've felt, I've seen
The rainbows edge
Lovely colors shine
They're beautiful… enticing too
But-that's another time.

Could

You don't know me
I don't know you
Our skins are different color
And this shines
Through
We work in
Different places
And all this
Shines thru
Our children too
Can see this too
And its all because
You don't know you
Maybe we should
Take time
To understand this
See it thru
So I could better
Get to know you
And
You could better
Get to
Know me too

A Port

All alone, all alone
All alone-
In a boat
On a timeless sea
Drifting, drifting
Drifting on
With none near,
Close by me.
Others far, far away
Near the world's-deep curve-
And them…
Very soon, I won't see.
All alone, all alone, all alone
In a boat-on a timeless sea,
Drifting, drifting
Drifting on.
To a port-
Not now known
To me.

What Is

What is love-what is love
Please tell me, what is love?
Is it the winds-thru the trees
The rustle of leaves.
The green of grass
Blossoms on trees
A family-the homeless
That live on the streets
The oceans the shores
Where tides come and go
Or is it in the secrets of-
Fascination too
Where secrets come and…
Then they slip thru.
And life goes on-creation does too
What is love-what is love
Please tell me-what is love?

Loves Creation

To be where one can
Plant a tomato
Touch a blossome
Dig in the soil
Clip a hedge
Smell of cut grass
As a mower moves by
See blue of sky
While lazy, creamy
White clouds drift by
Catch a ladybug-then…
Let it fly away
Get away from-the phone
Checkbook, email too
Just be-with the dandelions,
Bees, with creation-
Be free
Sometime for one
To be where one can do this-
Then do this
Is a most-also gives
A most-
Relaxing deep feeling
And a harvest…
From Loves Creation.
The very best.

Summer

Its Summer Time and,
Its July too
A time when nice things
Move swiftly thru
When a day of
Independence-is celebrated
With at night the heavens
A blaze-in human ways
And by day-with….
Food-picnic's and-
Popping, cracking
-Joyful ways,
All this and more
In lovely
Summer Time
When…
Its July too
At a time,
When nice things-
Creations things
Move-swiftly thru-is lovely.

Things To Do

On a hill its fun to play
On a blue and sunny day
Eat a hot dog
Spill your drink
Watch it slowly run away.
Or watch a rainbow in the sky
After a storm has past us by
And see the colors
That we see
Some we feel…
Like morning
In the sky.
Oh its sometimes nice to do.
Good things
You really,
Like to do.

Mysterious

The sea-the sea
Its lovely
Its beautiful
Its mysterious too
Its calm its rough
Its courageous too
Its friendly
Its unfriendly
It gives, it takes
Visits shores-feeds
Helps lives-it lives.
But will not be bridled
The sea-the sea
Its lovely-its beautiful
Mysterious too,
Its watched since, creation…
The world...pass thru.

Saved

Many little things-I've kept
And saved them-many for you
They're in my thoughts
The things I do...I've done.
And hope these souvenirs,
Keep sakes in my thoughts-
Treasured all these years.
Those many little things
You've seen me do.
I hope in some way…
They may help you.

One Step

Taking one step a day
If that's all
That you can do
Is slow… that's true
But keep on-keepin on
Taking one step a day
If that's all
That you can do-cause…
You'll get there too.

Don't

You don't know me
I don't know you
If we don't try
Now how can we
You might be good
I might be too
If we never know
How can good come thru
Only bad we see
We think that thru
And good we want too
All because…
I don't know you
And you don't
Know me.
How about that

See

Cant you see-cant you see
Cant you see-cant you see
Cant you see-the lady bug
With big black spots
Crawling-just crawling
Over there
What's wrong-just…
What's wrong with you people
Oh don't bother now
You scared it some how
But I just seen-
A lady bug-and…
A lot of happy pass by now.
Cant you see-cant you see

Good

Have a good time
Have it your way
Because you only come
One time this way.
So, have a good time
(in a good way)

It

I don't like it
I don't like it that way-
I don't like the way it looks,
It don't look the same
Anymore.
I like it like it was
Before
If it can't be the same
Somehow-
Not like it is now.
I don't like it
I just…
Don't like it.

Must Be

The waste can will be
Filled quick today
For the modern folk
Live in a different way
They live from cans
And boxes, and paper bags
They fill everything quick
That's around to be filled
The garbage cans, the
Waste baskets too will
Be filled quick today
All done in a comparable
Interesting progressing
Way
That must be
Very…
Thoughtfully-done
My goodness wow...
They're all-filled gone through
In just a few hours
Too.

A Crow

A bird-a crow
Came flying low
And in the bright
Sunlight.
Flew low-flew high
As the bird went by,
And then flew-
Out of sight.

Tonight

There's that June moon
Half round soon, full.
Near a bright star
Where-
Close by, others are,
And a few clouds
In a dark blue sky.
Tonight is so lovely
With only-
The moon, stars,
A few clouds
The sky-
And I, with…
The month
Of June-Junes moon…
Passing by

Everyday

Since you've left
I can see now…all…
The beautiful you've done-
And wish somehow
I could repay to you
But really…
Don't know how.
So just think-
That I'll more help others
And in this way
I'll help to spread
The love-you've spread
More and more,
Each day.
Thank you-thank you
Now I feel your love
Shines more bright,
More and more bright
With creation-
Since you've left…
Everyday.

Rolly Polly

I touched
A rolly poley
Crawling by,
And it curled in a circle
With only
One try.

Away

When its time to go
Please
Just slip away
And quietly…
Close the door
On this today.
So there will be
Just memory
Of today-yesterday
And of the then.
Left…
Creating, creating
The beautiful
To remember.
As you sail, sail, sail
Silently-silently
Into forever,
And love.
And with eternity
Away.

The Way

Having a silent protest
Don't know why…
Having it my way
No one else knows
didn't shave for three days
When I look in the mirror
I can look happy or mean
My reflection understands
And always agrees
Rub my beard…
Then I smile-
My reflection does too,
Now I'm thru.
Think I'll shave tomorrow
Happiness I know-
Will follow.
Having it my way.
Kind of-smoothes bumps
Along the way

Tell Me

Can you tell me
Just how
When you plant a seed
In the ground
Then it dies-and it grows
It can feed a bunch of people-
Those you know,
Those you don't know.
Can you make a seed
The same
If you can't-then…
Tell me who can
Tell me his name.
Cause-
That's quite a-marvelous,
Thing to do
And then…
See the whole thing
Thru.

That One

Ssssh-sssh-the snails,
Are racing-they just begun
My snails "that one"
The fat one-over there....
See it-the one on that side-
I think he won
My snail doesn't move fast
and moves pretty slow
But gets there fast
The way snails go.
And my snail-
The fat one, way over there
I think he won
Sssh-sssh-"wow"
What a snail race
And it just begun.

Do And Does

Does everything, every where know
When the sun will rise?
Do caterpillars know they-
Will be butterflies?
Do snowflakes know-
Sunrays are warm?
Do clouds know just,
How to make a storm?
Does twilight know of evening?
Does evening know of midnight?
Does midnight know of dawn?
Does everything everywhere know
When the sun will rise?
Do caterpillars know they-
will be butterflies?
Pss't......
If you know please-
Whisper to me, and....
I will tell everybody
Then we'll all know.
Thank You.

Below

Buried with a bell to ring
If you hear
A-ding a ling
Dig a hole, real fast,
And say hello-
Hey..
How are you?
Way down below

New Ways

To bite the bullet
come up with new
over here-over there
Create new ways
to approach light
Of days- to lead
To follow-to respect
The shallow-the full
The whole of mankind
All kinds of
Positive thinking
Is beautiful,
Is lovely
Is watched by many
Admired-hated
Envied.
To be able
To bite the bullet
And to...
See things thru

Helping

There are-
Many ways to help
To sing, many ways
To sing lifes song
As we move along.
We could sing-
We could dance-
We could walk
With each other-
We could listen
We could read
We could help
Along the way
In small ways
We might think
That is nothing
But is large
like a mountain
When needed
by others-much
In need a long-
The way.
Helping others
Is so lovely
And helps one too
Eternally
There are many-
Many ways
Much as sunshine
And blue skies
To help each other-
If we...but try

A Snail

Hey,
I got a snail
And you don't have one
I got a snail
Betcha wish you had one
You can't have the
Snail I got.
Cause I got the snail
And you do not
Ha-ha

How Bout You

TV tells me what to do
Seven days of
Scheming and friends
All week.
Five days of school
Every week
6 hours of church
And the golden rule
Dad works
Mom works too
Seems they just
Come home cause
That's the thing to do.
TV and friends
Most tell me
What to do.
How bout you?

Society

If in the sky
Sometime you go
Where sky is blue
And drifting clouds are white.
Is blue ok with you
Or drifting clouds
Of white all right.
Or maybe...
Just to stay between
The blue and white
Would that be the same?
While you study-from on high
With you...
If in the sky
Sometime you go-please
call and tell us
Where you be –in that high
Society,
And...
Thanks

Hour

Once a hour
Is lost in a day
Its seems to go
Its own special way.
(To return)
Never returns again
In the same day.
So do what's to be done
With the rest
Of the day.

Mixed

The sun came up-the moon came too
The stars came out-the clouds come too
And then the milky way
The clouds-the dark
And dawn-oh the dawn
That brought a morning
Of sun-a noon-a beautiful
Lovely twilight and evening,
Night-midnight too…
And the sun-the sun
I don't know why
I don't know why
Tho…
The sun all mixed
With twilight
Keeps mixed…
And shining thru-for me from yesterday.
In– memories…way.

Before The Snow

My friends the robins have returned
They left last fall
You know…
Right before the snow.
I seen them this morning
Right after sun-up
The very first day of spring
With their orange breast
And gray black colored
Topside.
Just the two
Maybe they're the same pair
That was here last year.
They were looking at the pine trees
Near the fence line
I guess to make a nest
And raise a family
Its sure nice to know winter's finished
Spring is here
And my friends have returned.
I seen them this morning
Right after sun-up
Just the two
You know
They left last fall
Right before the snow.

Most Times

Way over in the corner
Of the fence line.
There is an old pine tree
With some grass near it
And some sand there too.
And, the grass has-
A sinking spot
That seems to stay
All day thru-
And, all night too,
You can see it.
By the old pine tree
Way…over in the corner
Of the fence line.
Where its… kind of
Lonesome like too-
Most times.

For You

Now that you've hit-
Your stride
go inside a little more
Treasures wait for you
They are stored-
The key is in your heart
It must feel the need
The love-to feed
The certain feel
The really real...
To open your hearts door
Where your-only your
True, help, honest help
For you, lies...
Now that you've hit your stride
go inside and ride-
With loves
Lovely ride...that waits deep inside for you.

Be

To see the world
Thru children's eyes
How different that would be
The things we see-and how we see
The things they see and how they see
How different they would be
The things that are good
And things that are bad
Perhaps they might be good
Or maybe not so bad
Or maybe bad-but
A little good.
And maybe with a little
Fixing and things might
Be– or be a little bit better
And with maybe not
So much fighting and a
Little more talking
Like children do
Like children still do.
Maybe...to see
The world thru
children's eyes...
How different that would or could perhaps be.

Where

Don't follow me
I don't know where I'm going
I'm going over here
I'm going over there
I'm going over there
Here, around in circles
And everywhere
Jumping, running
Walking too
Any way to just
To get where I really
Want to
How about you?
Where are you going?

Water

Cold, cold water
And hot water too
Tastes really good
If its
Time for it to

My Treat

I can almost be you but never complete
Because I am me
And always will be
That is my treat
No matter what-
We go thru
This will always
Be true
I can almost be you
But never complete
I am me-
That is my treat

The Package

Teeth-teeth
Everybody has em
They came in the package
With you
Clean em-
Take care of em
They'll help you
If you do
And make your food
Taste good
As you-
Chew-chew-chew
Teeth-teeth-teeth
Everybody has em
Keep em too
Cause they came
In the package
With you

See

Oh a snake
In the grass
Is hard to see
But its there.
And if a snake
A snake-a snake
I really must see.
A snake in the open
Is the snake for me.
There the snake
Can see me-
And the snake
I can see.

A Nice Day

Today has been a very nice day
The sun is nearly gone today-twilight too-
And evening, for a while, is here to stay
The moon is round and full
The sky deep dark and blue
With no clouds to see in view
If you were here-and with me now
maybe you too would say somehow
That...
Today has been a very nice day.

Make Best

Reimaging
Look deep inside
Where all good faith
Should there abide
Tho think things thru
In what we do
To change and alter
As we do
And strive too
Do the most good
As we pass thru
Reorganize
If that must be
To make the best
Of what we see.

Came

Christmas has came
And gone this year
It brought its Christmas cheer
To me there was much
To think about
Some good, some bad
Some just about,
The times that happen
As we live thru the years...as they
Come and go.
And take us a long
With the song of life
As it comes-and we
See it go-near the end of year.

Strange

Isn't it strange what bodies do-
As age comes along
And we grow
We grow daily and strong
Then comes time to grow-
As age strokes us
Along.
And then we grow
Small first larger
Soon walk-slower
Small-old and walk-slow,
Isn't it strange
What age can do
To almost-
everything

Summer Time

Now that it's summer time
Oh for the summer time
When we can keep the house
As cold as it was-
In the winter time,
And not complain,
Oh for the summer time
Ain't we grand
For this to understand.
Summer time-
Like we do.

How

Should acquaintances of old
have the modern touch
should they have the fast
like aero planes
and streamlined trains
and cars-plus hydroplanes
or should they only have
horse drawn wagons
oxen too
with slow of carts
they often drew
and high wheeled
bicycles
oil lamps too
And log cabins-for houses
from trees they chopped
down
building houses and towns
or...
should acquaintances of old
have the modern touch
or should it remain
as old
to be told
as such
How should this be?
For memories
To hear... and-
see.

School Days

School days
School days
School days
Walking
Bikin
Skatin
Ridin
To school
School days
School days
Vacation days
Learning too
School days
School days
Graduation day
School days
School days
School days
Goin-Goin
Gone
Work days-work days
Here to stay.

People

Worry, worry, worry
And yet, most people do.
Worry, worry, worry
Now just what does it do?
Does it help in loving ways?
Does it brighten up the day?
Does it really push clouds away?
Does it make the sunshine thru?
Now just what does it do?
Worry, worry, worry
And yet... most people do.

Bumped

He bumped his head
He bumped his head
The little boy
He bumped his head
When he jumped
on the jungle gym
He hit his head
on a pipe and he
bumped his head
He cried a little too
Everyone came to see
what did he do
when he bumped his head
when he bumped his head
on the jungle gym
They came to see
Just what ...
had
Happened to him.

Moving

I see clouds moving
Slow in the sky
The wind -
I think the wind,
Is moving the clouds
I cannot see the wind
can you see the wind?
But I see clouds
Moving across the sky
and the sky is blue
maybe the wind
is blowing the clouds
To a pocket in the sky
To stay
for cloudy days.
I see clouds moving
Slow...
To somewhere
somewhere,
in the sky.

Everyday

Since you've left
I can see now...all…
The beautiful you've done-
And wish somehow
I could repay to you
But really…
Don't know how.
So just think-
That I'll more help others
And in this way
I'll help to spread
The love-you've spread
More and more,
Each day.
Thank you-thank you
Now I feel your love
Shines more bright,
More and more bright
With creation-
Since you've left…
Everyday.

Asking

Thanks for looking asking…
How are you?
That to me-means-
You in some way know
For you've been there too
And know-
Also can understand,
What I'm now going thru.
Thanks for looking
Asking.
And…
Thanks again
It has a golden touch
In means much.

Smooth

"Oh"… its down hill now
Just as smooth
As it can be
Ain't no hills in sight
Least none that
I can see
I can glide along
And sail
Just as free as free can be
Cause…
Its down hill now
Just as smooth
As smooth can be.

Time Less

We may never know
Just how, the lives we live
Or the things we do
Or the gifts we give
May have too effect
On the lives of others
Or, the lives we live.
Isn't it strange
How our secrets made
In someway rhyme,
With timeless-
Time…-just why-
We may never know.

Christmas

Then Christmas in
Its way
Brought love and joy
In a special way when it came this year
And moved silent-
On its way.
Leaving bundles of
Blessings
Beautifully bound-
To thank about.

Life's Road

Along life's road
There's rocks-there's trails
There's trees-there's green
There's fences-there's clouds
There's blue of sky
There's the silent place
Where memories
Are built too…
Along life's road,
As you –pass thru.

A Day

I lost a friend today
I lost an entire day
I thought today was Saturday
But found today was Sunday
And I had plans for today
Was going to go to church today
But thoughts got in my way
And new years then came too
Mixing, mixing my point of view
Oh well the new years
Right here too-with many many days
For others use-my use too.
But… I lost a friend today,
I lost... an entire day.

Changed

All has changed
As if arranged
But will be better
-Just wait and see
For will be.
As a blessing
That in time
Will shine
Eternally…
for you
As arranged
From far.

Tell

Tell the people
Tell the people
Tell the people
If its true
Tell the people
Tell the people
Even if it-is not true.
Tell the people
Tell the people
They'll believe you
If you do.

Tell Me

An orange
On an apple tree?
An apple on
An orange tree?
Perhaps this will
Never-ever-be
Because…
The two are not the same
An apple is an apple
And an orange is an orange
If ever on the
Same tree
These two there you see
Please, please…
Come run and tell me.

A Ball

I seen a ball
So very big
So very big-and it was green
The more I looked
The more I seen
And all I seen
Was more green, green.

A Member

What some folks
Worry about
Just don't seem-
To matter much, to others
And what others
Worry about
Just don't seem to matter
Much-to some
It seems worry
Comes to all-in,
Different ways.
Then rears its head
Is felt-
For days and days
In its own way
When it leaves-its remembered
In memory
As the face of
An undesired
Member
Of
Life's, history.

To Me Listen

Listen to me
I'm the wind
There's no other
Sound around
Only me-only me
Only me-you can hear
No one near
None other-none other
Just listen to me
Listen to me
Listen to me
I'm talking to you
Let me thru
Let me thru
Listen-listen-listen
Listen to,-me-eee

Play

On a hill-not far away
Where grass is nice
And deep dark green.
Children play-
And can be seen.
Bouncing balls, flying kites
Playing, singing, having-
Just lots and lots
Of fun.
On a hill not far away,
Where children play

The Blossoms

After the blossoms
The flowers
And hours-and hours
Of beautiful
Then seeds come
go away
To start a brand new day
Of blossoms
Beautifully different…
All over again

Airplane

I seen an airplane
Flying by
Up in the sky, so blue
Where it was going
I don't know
For if I did
I could tell-
Would you?

Change

Revolution
Revolution
Change in motion
Revolution-revolution
A piece of history
A brand new story
Revolution-revolution
Can this be
Good or bad
What we see
Now would you please
Tell me why…
A solution
To…
The revolution.

Thanks

A half moon
In-June-I see
With stars nearby
Popping out
All over the sky.
A cloud over here
Way over there too
All this passing thru
You've just seen
With me.
A lovely half moon
Stars a deep dark sky
On a quiet night
In June.
Thanks, wow-
Lucky me.

Empty Sails

The emptiness -
It still prevails
as sailing ships with
empty sails
That drifts quite lifeless
along on silent sea
not moving far - but moving on
on and listless on
day by day by endless
endless day,
Till comes the day
The breeze that blows
Tho slightly blow it may
and sails that fill ever slight
The ship it shudders
light it does then slow
It moves, along, along, along,
and on to the open
silent sea...
on, on , and on
As if - in quiet song
To a rythmn
a rythmn of old
a rythmn of new
Till sails with silence
fill...
Speaking old - yet
with
a sense of new
wonderfully
sailing memories
too
A sailing ship - on a silent sea
moves ghostly, silently - with...
a silent crew...moves-
Ever, ever, and...on.

Ago

I remember the time
I remember it well
Happened in a small - one room
School house long time ago in Michigan
One boy said, other's laughed
You like that little girl
with the long black hair
she likes you too -
We can see it from here
I was small - so was she
I wanted to hit him - so did she
we were both small - maybe
6 - 7 or so, a long time ago
weeks, months, years go by
like birds that fly
I wonder where the little girl is
The one boy that said she likes you too
The others that laughed
Even the school house its
gone too - wonder where they are?
cause...
I remember the time
I remember it well
Its only been, a little over -
seventy years ago.
Maybe a little more,
or so.

It's Cool

Its cool- its cool
Its real cool
And-
Kind of windy today
The birds- only a few
Are flying today
It must be cool
In the air
To the birds
When they fly today too.
Of course
I don't know-but-
Its cool- its cool
And...
Kind of windy,here-
Today.

So Many

I see
Flat clouds
Round clouds
White clouds
Grayish clouds
Cloudy clouds
Scattered clouds
Many, many, many clouds
All under a
Sky of sunshine,
Blue
If you were here
And see
What I see.
You could see
All I see
Too.

Hazy

The sun is shining
Its cloudy too
The sky is kind of
Hazy blue
With the sun shining
The sky hazy blue
Most folks think
Today`s
A nice day,
Too.

Cloudy Today

Its cloudy- its cloudy
Real cloudy today
The sky is blue
But clouds hide it
Away
An air plane
I hear flying
Way over the clouds
High in the sky
Where the sky is all blue
But I cannot see it
Clouds hide it away the sun it is shining
High up where the sky is all blue-but,
Its hazy hazy, hazy
Here today
Clouds, hide...
The sun away.
Its cloudy too. Its cloudy
Real cloudy today
And maybe it will
Be cloudy- for...
The rest, of the
Day.

The Sky

Tonight there's
A lonesome full moon
In the sky.
If you look close tho
There's stars all over
Too-in the sky.
Together they light up
The deep dark
Mysterious heaven high.
With tonight's lovely
Full moon in the sky.

A Breeze

My what a gentle caressing breeze…
And then it was gone
Like the notes of a-
Nearly forgotten song.
Perhaps it was-a breeze
Of that kind
Simply…
A caressing breeze
Left-
From another time.

At Times

Pictures you sometime want
Have a way
Of quietly slipping away
Where you can never
Find them,
Where they choose
To stay.
It seems at times
Forever-forever
And a day…
Their way

Away

Where did the clouds go
I can see blue of sky today
I can see sunshine too
Now that the clouds
Have gone away,
It makes the world
Seem crisp and clear
I can almost hear
The beautiful softly say
All is ok
Please look see-its lovely again
Now that the clouds
Have gone away.

Moonlight-Sunlight

The moon it is
So bright tonight
It looks like
A morning of
Clear sunlight
And the trees
And houses
Look so near
Tho they are far
They seem right here.
The mountains
I know they
Are far, so far away
But tonight
They look dark
And real nice
In this light like day.
When folks walk by
And they say hello
They look kind
Of strange
in the moonlight glow
Because the
Sunlight knows
And the moonlight knows
How to light
Everything

cause they were

Taught just how

When only creation

Was modeling

Imagine

Other planets
Are so far away
And sometime
Seem so near
They look like
Bright lights
In the sky
Or sometime
Like an
Airplane passing
By.
Or things we can
Imagine
Way-high
Up, in the sky

Mornings

Today mornings late… Does it ever
Seem like that
To you?
Sometime…
Yes of course
It seems like
That to me,
Golly-ghee.
Mornings come strange
At times.

Not The Same

Christmas is coming
And will soon be here
It's not quite the same
As it was last year.
At least to me-
From what I now see.
For the one that helped
For years and years
Is ill this year.
And watches and shares
In a special way-
We all can feel,
With approaching days.
Because…
Christmas is coming
All the holidays too
But not quite the same-
At least to me (except in love)
As the days pass thru-
Like stars…
In the heavens above.

Controlled

We are controlled
By the mind
In all that we do
Whether big or small
Good or bad
Simple or brilliant.
Not by the muscles
Cause they only do
What the mind
Tells them to.
All of the time
The thoughts
Of the mind
The thoughts
Or the mind
We are controlled
By the mind
In all we do
All of the time.

Mr. Snail

Hey Mr. Snail
With your house on your back
Where are you going?
And when are you coming back?
If you see a little sunshine
Shining on your way
Hey Mr. Snail
You will have a fine day

Of Spring

In the winter months
There is to see
No leaves upon
Most any tree.
But in the spring
Spring rains will bring
Buds and leaves
And flowers of spring.

Love

We speak of love
But what is love
Is it the same for you-for me?
Is it the same for me-for you?
This of course-we must think thru.
A mothers love, tho-
Is much the same
All life time thru.
For the family, and children too, feel that-
The mother is there with love, to correct,
and to see them thru,
In what they do.
And a mothers love, is true
All the way
A lifetime thru.
So a mothers love
Is really love, a lovely love.
For a mothers love
Never finishes-its never done.
Because mothers, children
Family too-if they to each
Are truly true...
They love, as one.

For now

Go away
Stay away from me-go away
go way-go away-please,
Please-please go away.
I want to see you
I want to see you
I don't want to see you
I hate you-I love you
Please go away
Please go away
I've seen you before
For years-for years
You went away-you went away
I lost you-I forgot you
I see you-I want you
But please go away
I don't know why, I love you
go away just go away-for now...

Something

There's a something
in the atmosphere
That fills December days
A feel a glow
That inside kind of
Changes folk'ses ways.
Perhaps...its
The crisp of air
The neon Lights
With children...tinsel everywhere.
Small bells that chime
To bring the time
Of Christmas
Closely near.
And birth a special day
Just filled with love
That fills
The atmosphere
Of wishing -everyone
Just everywhere...
A very
Merry Christmas
And, a...
Lovely-Happy New Year.

Soccer Game

Soccer is a nice game
A very nice game
To play.
You kick the ball
This way
You kick the ball
That way.
Whoops over the fence
I seen the ball go.
No more soccer ball today.

Varying Memories

With another
Close but far - alone almost
Were the two thru
The years
And separated slightly
As stars on high
While years went by
The storms came - sunshine
More storms relentless, changing
Almost unbearable at times
Assistance from storms,
Most family storms
Not around- available - storms
Not any where around
Permanent-
To be found.
One violent storm
Completely destroyed
One of the two
While memories flow- at times
For the other, of two.
Remaining alone, close but far
Separated by far
As stars, on high above
That drift with
Varying memories
Of love- drift
In silent... by.

Years Ago

Yuh-know
many many years ago
When I was young
Back in my teens
A young adult - there
Somewhere in between
When I'd see older folks
or folks walkin slow
white hair on top
and you'd hear - see
other folks step aside
and say,
Hi Mr. Brown or hello Mrs. Jones
How are you folks today,
I'd look, and to myself
I'd say,
I'll never get old
Not me- not me- not me
I'll never get old
But look, look, look - and know
At the story, I told -
cause...
I'm old.

Place

White flowers
Orange flowers
Green grass too
Grow on a hillside
With green trees-
Drifting clouds,
Neath a hazy sky of blue.
Where children play-
Folks grow-passing years away
I think, I think
Oh yes I really do.
That's a most beautiful place
To leave, come, stay, play,
Where-
White flowers, orange flowers
Green grass too
Grow on a hillside
Forever on a hillside... just...
there with you

75

Immortalizing

Gone from the sky
Is the light of the sun
soon after twilight of evening
evenings twilight
But sunlight returns
with light of dawn
for sunlight lives on - as momories of rocks do
Rocks and memories
They... both seem- They seem as forever- they do.
Immortalizing...
memorializing sunlight.
For-
Tho gone from the sky
soon after each evenings twilight
The
sunlight forever returns
at dawn,
with light eternally
also lovely
as the,
creations-
creations light, A beautiful light
A light - of, love.

Drops

Rocks so massive
Tall and large
Forming entire
Mountainsides
Can be cracked and fall
Tremendously...
From small drops
Of water
Drying, freezing,
Thawing, expanding
Thru the years
So silently are the
Small, small,
Drops of water
Causing rocks
To split and fall-on,
Our mountainsides
Tremendously

A Sailing Slip

One Evening
They sailed from the port
to far, far away
Thru the waters of the
ocean - Thru its waves
To the far away
Right before twilight of evening
Right before close of day
Till the ship - a sailing ship
sailed with sails at full
to a mere speck in the waves
where the sky meets the sea
at the horizon
to its disappearing
The ship sailed on forever on -
At full sail
fading
gradually, finally
wonderfully , beautifully
as daylight leaves
the sky after
a lovely, lovely
sunset
the ship sailed - it sailed
from view
from port
to the far, far
never to be seen again -
away
lovely... silently
away.

The Wall

There's a shadow
On the wall
From the sunshine far away
That looks like
It's came to stay.
But will disappear today
When the sun has moved away
My shadow on the wall
My shadow on the wall
I seen it-I seen it
I know, I know, I know, I know
I know, I know, "I know" I seen it
But maybe…
It wasn't there to stay-
At all.

A Nice Day

Today, I think-will be a nice day
For the clouds are slow,
Moving away.
And sunshine-with sky of blue
Is shining bright thru.
Yes, today-I think, for me-
Will be, a very nice day.
And may be for you too,
Your way.

Blue

Hazy blue the mountains-of,
Far away
Under a hazy blue
Of sky
Make a hazy lazy
Afternoon
A soft beautiful
Most lovely way.

Your Way

Maybe its best
You remember it
Your way
That's the way
You seen it
All the time
That's the way
Its best
Its sublime
That way
And maybe everyday
It don't hurt nobody
That way
Maybe its best
You remember it
Your way
All the time...
Your way

Miracles

Touching in a way
As mornings sunrays
Does a day.
Music does the soul
And remains
There forever
Like moonlight
On water, does
To the memory.
Stepping ever
So lightly music
Touches in silent
Thunderous but
Lovingly speaks
Leaves –spiritual
Eternal,
Daily and always
Feelings-filling
Quite as
Morning sunrise
and moonlight
Miracles.
Helping Touching
In ways we hardly
Understand
Thru and with
Our creators
Constant loving
Eternal Touch– of
Just, lovely.

An Agreement

If there's a war-and,
Your house is mine-and
You live in the basement-and
I live up stairs-
You raise your family there
I raise my family upstairs
We live that way for years
Does that make all right
Thru love
Tho peace may appear
As clouds and sunshine above
Or does this remain
Because of time war
Or is it now-or might it
Remain-a cause of great
Pain-
Me upstairs-and you down below
In the basement as an agreement of war-
Long long ago.

Be

To see the world
Thru children's eyes
How different that would be
The things we see-and how we see
The things they see-and how they see
How different they would be.
The things that are good
And things that are bad
Perhaps they might be good
Or maybe not so bad
Or maybe-just...
Just a little good.
And maybe with a little
Fixin things might be,
or be-a little bit better.
And with maybe-just maybe
Not so much fightin
A little more talkin
Like children do-
Like children still do.
Maybe to see-the world thru
Children's eyes..
How different that would-or could...
Perhaps be.

78

Hug

Very few give a hug
For free anymore-
Just what has happened
And what's in store
for those who hug
As those did before.
When a hug-was a hug
Given with love
In Store.
That was free-like...
A breeze soft-on...
A spring filled day.
Oh, say-what has happened?
For it seems few, very few

Give just an old fashioned hug.
That felt free and lovely
And embraceable...too-and gave..
Like a hug-like a hug-like a hug
Is really supposed to-do.

Most Times

Way-over in the corner
Of the fence line.
There is an old pine tree
With some grass
Near it and-
Some sand there too
And the grass and the sand has,
A sinking spot
That seems to stay
All day thru-and,
All night too. You can see it.
By the old pine tree-way...
Over in the corner
Of the fence Line
Where its... kind of
Lonesome like too...most times.
By that fence line,
Near that sinking spot-
And the old pine tree.

Lonesome

Hospital halls-are lonesome
Tho filled with many folks
They have a feeling of-
Stay if you come
As long as you please
We're here to make better,
Your day.
And in halls of this kind
You may feel that they say
Leave, Leave this is no place
For you.
We'll call-we'll call
Come only then.
But come, but come
And stay with us then
We welcome you here
There is space,
For you here.
Now is early you must wait
And come then.
Oh, hospital halls are the
Most lonesome of halls
You don't seem to fit there,
To stay... tho they're filled-
Till you're called.

Dripping

Dripping water
And falling rain
Are almost—
But not quite,
The same

Thoughts

When you're lost
And really don't-
Know where to go
Blend with the fishes
Of deep and go where they go
Where you seldom peep
Just lose your thoughts
In waters deep
Where only the fish
Doth reside
And you'll find
it friendly there,
There in thought
To reside
For there silence
Always is near
The sounds of earth
Rare appear
The fish going deep
They go by
Even the birds there
Don't Fly-they just float
Quietly by
Day light dark
Pass quiet too
When it's time
For this act-to be true.
Yes, by all means
When you're lost
And really don't
Know where to go
In your thoughts.
Blend with fishes of deep-and...
Go where you seldom peep.

I See You

I see you
But you don't see me
Cause when you're angry
You only see.
The very tiny things
That you want to see

Mystery

Hazy blue
And twilight too
Will soon bring
Stars of night
And mysterious
Moonlight
Silently-quietly
Dark,
Of mystery
Soon
Very soon
For
You.
As shades of evening
Flows
Just lovely
Thru.

You

Pause and reflect
In the light
Of the you-
You see
In the mirror
All see-
Where they view
In a mirror
Themselves
And tell me why
-Just why
Thru your moments
When you-
Pause and reflect on
Why-just why
You are-
The marvelous
You
You think you are.
That....you do.
While you
Are passing
Thru.

Old

Everything
Gets old
That's they way
The stories told
Cats get old
Dogs get old
Horses cows and
People too
It happens as
We all pass thru
Everything, I mean-
Everything,
It all gets old
For-that's the way
Its stories told.
Everything gets old.
Everything gets old.
Passing-passing
Passing thru
And that's the way
Its suppose to be
For everyone
And all
To see.
Even you-
And me.

Time

Time is with us-it is with us
Every where we go
We can not see it
We can not hear it
It is silent as in spirit
But is is there
It is with us-everywhere
We go.
It makes us old-
It makes us young
It makes us think
As song we've sung
Tho we can not make
Even a second of time.
And love is there
In all of time.
If we but seek...
With love-with time
In our time-
Our given time.
For...
Time is with us-it is with us
Everywhere we go.

Beautiful

A little clouds
A little rain
A little sunshine
And a rainbow too
Makes a beautiful day
For you
And me too.

Butterfly's

Two white butterfly's
Two white butterfly's
Flying round an apple tree
Happy I think as they can be.
Two white butterfly's
Two white butterfly's
And...
I think they're looking right at me.

Everyone

Music-music-music
Music has a way
To bring something
To the dark
Something to the light
A something in a way
That lifts us
Lowers us
Enlightens us
Awakens us
Music that we understand
Music that we don't
Music, music, music
Has a silent way
To send a love
To everyone
In...
An individual, way

A Time

There's a time
In the midnight hour
A time in the daylight too
When the silence
Of true
Comes thru to you
In beautiful light
That only you
Can comprehend.
And this is love
That you must share
For its from deep...
Deep, deep within
If you-in true
Asked from the light
Of love
Within.

Mapped

I Think...
Life is mapped
A certain way
That you live
From day to day
Choices are there
That you make
Of right or wrong
That you do-
As notes of song.
Then you reach
The mountains
Low or high
As you travel along
I think-
Life is mapped
A certain way
From day to day.

Children

You are trusted
By a child
Once you have
Earned their
Respect.
And once-
you have earned it,
Children never
Forget it.

Maybe

We sure ain't
What we used to be
Neither you nor I,
We're scattered
Like clouds
That hang low
In the sky.
Some wide as can be
Some thin-
Like a tree.
Just look at us now
We ain't the-
Same somehow.
We sure ain't-
What we used to be
Maybe...
Maybe-come to think of it-
Maybe we ain't-....
S'pose-to be.

To See

If..
You like this
And I like that
And you like this
And we can't see
That its okay
If you like this
And I like that
That we behave
In such a way
and others see
This every day
They soon will think
And they will say
A little love would help
These folks to see
Its very small things
On which...
They disagree

Today

You I see, from far away
Thru the eyes of a camera
Given me today,
Thru technology.
And I can destroy-the you,
I see with bombs,
And psychology.
From thousands of miles,
Away-If I so choose...
Or help you.
Either way...
The choice in my mind
I see-
Its up to me.
Isn't it incredible
Or-is it terrible.
The things we have
Learned to do today
To our friends or others
We can see-or converse
With-from so far -far
Far away

Yellow Butterfly

There goes a butterfly
And its yellow too
There goes a butterfly
Quiet, flying by.
Yellow butterfly
Yellow butterfly
Yellow butterfly
Bye bye.

For You

When we want green
Of fields
And lovely waters–calm and still
And storms
With clouds-
Of dark appear.
Creating fear-just lonesome chill.
Remember sunshine
Crystal skies of blue-with time
Shine thru-and
Beautiful rainbows too
After storms… thru
Faith, hope, love
Fulfilling forgotten wishes
Creating creations
Large fields of love with-
Sun come, glowing
Never small...
For you- come,thru,

Me-You

P'sst hey,
What is it that you
Like to do.
You can tell me-
I won't tell if you do.
Me... I like to
Collect calendars
Have 2 or 3 in one
Room–any where I like,
All over the place...
That's what I like-
I really do
What is it that you
Like to do?
You can tell me
I won't tell...
"Wh, oops"-
I told you,
Scuse me.

Slow-Slow

Sunshine halfway
Up the mountain
Cloudy rest way to the top
Sunshine moved up
Slow slow
Guess it'll never stop.

To Be

From small of age
What we-
Believe to be.
From medium of age
What we believe
To be.
From large of age
What we believe
To be.
From full grown
of age-what we
Believe to be.
Is...hard to change
And what we
Think, and see-feel
And be-
Forms-much of
What we are.
And like a star
As how we shine
In creation
Where we are.

A Season

Easter brings a season
Of suffering and respect
Of deep love and adoration
For love in silence too
That always is-
With and always stays
As the season
Of our deep
Respect
That the creator
Thru Easter
Always gives
And brings
Memorably
Easter season.

You

I found you (my wife)
In a country far away
And brought you
To my country-one fine day.
And happy we have been
Here far away.
We found our home
Raised a family-have grandchildren
Great grandchildren too.
The days have grown long…
And years so have they.
Tho in it all… No matter what
Each day or year
I brought you here-
And here we'll always be
in this country-now both ours…
Growing old, more lovely
Every day.

Touch

The winds touched
In a beautiful way
And lightened the
Feel of the morning
That day.
The touch of the ocean
As the tide came in
Was lovely to children
And all as it flowed in
Changing-all
On each shoreline
It touched
To never be the same while-the tide
Was in.
For the tide
Gives rules by which
All must abide while-
The touch of creation which-
Gives all in a way
That lives and breathes
The air of Each day
A special touch
Like the light of the sun
That has likes
As sunrays
From creation
With love.

Possible

In winter I believe
Summer will come.
When lost I believe
There's still a way
If you till, plant seeds, and water
The ground I believe
A seed will grow.
I believe that after storms
A rainbow will come
And light the sky
And birds will fly.
I believe a small candle lit
Placed in the dark
Will light the dark with
Silent love.
I believe love brings lovely.
I believe faith brings
Lasting wonders.
I believe love and faith
Is wondrous, spiritual
And eternal
In winter I believe
Summer will come
In the dark I believe
The sun will shine.
I believe thru belief
And love and faith.
The impossible
That is possible...
Is possible

Honors

A honorable
Occupation
Whatever it may be
Gives occasion and a reason
Whenever
The season-
To beautiful
Honors, be
In lovely
ways

Before The Snow

My Friends the robins have returned,
They left last fall
You know...
Right before the snow.
I seen them this morning
Right after sun-up
The very first day of spring
With their orange breast
and gray black colored
Topside.
Just the two
Maybe they're the same pair
That was here last year.
They were looking at the pine trees
Near the fence line
I guess to make a nest
And raise a family.
Its sure nice to know winters finished
Spring is here
and my friends have returned.
I seen them this morning
Right after sun-up
Just the two
You know
They left last fall
Right before the snow.

Me

A bird, a crow
On a light post
Near a shaggy
Old palm tree.
-Just a bird
-Just a crow
-Just a light post
And a shaggy-
Old plam tree.
But I seen this-
In the morning's quiet…
And, twas me.

The News

We heard the news
just heard it today
that the sunshine
is shining
real real bright today
that the sky is blue
about all over today
that children are playing
having great fun
playing - playing -
playing in the sun.
Tho the skies blue
a few clouds
are around
Down way down low
near the ground.
Also...
We heard it today
you may be gone for -
a few days.
We wish you creations
most lovely, lovely
Blessings
with bright sunshine,
in most - beautiful, ways.

The Bird

A bird can fly
we know not how
or why-for sure,
A few may know
for sure - not I.
Because...
The wings move little
and...
The bird from stop
flies fast
Almost top speed
that lasts and lasts
with little movement
by the wings
or with great
movement of the wings
the bird flies much
the same it seems
Just where does,the-
bird, or fly, or bee
get such great speed
from stop or slow
they have - that be
a few may know,
for sure - not me.

To Hear

Most times when
Music-you hear
You listen,with a
Listening ear.
Folks like-to hear
Most times,
What music, has to say.
Most any time.
Most any
Night or day.

Found Underground The Miners

continues ...Found Underground The Miners

The eyes of the- world
shine on you
from where you've been-for what you've done
stayed away from
the world underground-in a mine,collapsed-
deep, deep underground
with no light around
for days and days
almost 18 days
with no outside sounds
and no light around
with friends of many
all deep so deep
underneath the ground
near... far away-
Then you were found
thru love which is felt
from above also deep,
deep and thru out,
every where around.
And is felt in creation
of the all, silent very
silent never, ever, leaves
where ever one goes is
always around, found with you
all others and friends
above, friends below
with love thru love
found a way thru lovely
with creations guidance
too. To let you know
that everywhere the
eyes of the world and
love thru love, family
love and all, never
forgot tho you were
away far far away

deep deep under the earth
for days and days 68 days
A way was found
thru creations love
to contact you
bring light
bring needs bring love
bring you, back to
above - with those
"(In the tube the phoenix - one by one)"
to those you love

Oh yes,
The eyes of the world
shine on you
with heavens light
like the sun, moon,
stars above
with eternal -
lovely love.

10/12/10

For miners
found in collapsed mine
brought back rescued Feb.
by tube

Far Away

I called to you
From in distance
Far away
And you answered
From the distance
Of far away
Tho your face
I could not see
From where you then be
I could tell
From the way
Your voice sounded
That day
You were not, as happy
Or smiling
The way you smile, happy
On most days.
When I called to you
From in distance
Of, far away.

For You

If the sky is blue
And
The sun is bright
And green grass
With every thing
Around
Is shining bright
In sunlight
Its a beautiful day
If you want it
To be
And all for you
Enjoy it too
Its here for you
With a sky of blue
Bright sunshine
Too...
Lucky, fortunate you.
All this
So beautiful
All for you.

Majestically

The dawn has came
In such a way
It slowly is
Tucking the moon away
I can see it tho
At its perch...
High in the sky
Majestically reigning
Beautifully by.
But the dawn has came
In such a way
It is slowly hiding
The moon with day.
Till comes the night
When the moon will rise again
In the open sky
And rule over the world
By night
With the stars
Nearby.

Clouded Blue

Its cloudy today
And the distant
Clouded hills
Are so blue dark blue
Today
They seem almost
A clouded dark blue black
In distant color
Creating a most beautiful
Colorful lovely
And mountainous view
Of clouded dark blue
On the hills,
Today.

Age

The rat race
The rat race
Where did it fly?
Age took the rat race
When age
Came by
And age never flies
You have it- always,
To contend with
Its way
Gradually- slowly
Bye bye rat race...
Hi age.

Way

Off to the club or,
The quiet go he
To hear the last word
In the quiet for he
In the house knows
The lady of the house
That in there stays.
Has the last word
Her way... always,
So off to the club
Or quiet goes he.
To have the last word
Sometime- his way,
Alcoholicly- and...
Quietly.

For Folks

If water melon's
Tasted like chocolate
All chocolaty, water melon- ney
Nice and sweet
And apples tasted like
Bubble gum,
Made bubbles- while
Apples, you eat
And oranges grew with straws
So you could drink orange juice
While oranges you eat
Wouldn't they be neat
To eat most anytime
For folks like you...
And yes- of course
Me too.
To eat
Most any old time
We just
Wanted too.

Away

Follow the line
Follow the line
Accelerate now
Accelerate- accelerate
To 60 or more
Till you're up off
And away
In to the night or day
Then climb climb, climb
Level the ship
And you're sailing off
Off
into the
Far- far away.

To You

When some memories
Come thru
Sort thru
Keep some close
To you
For its hard telling
What some memories
Could do
Twisted by others
That you give them to.
So...
When some memories
Come thru
Keep em...
Close to you.

Fence's

Fence's on roadside
Seem to guide
In a way
Ones way
From roadside.
As one travels
On ones way
Along life's road,
Fenced and
Guided feelings
Along life's road-create,
Maybe, question-
Of which way.

Chase

When you chase
The moon
And think
You have it
Because it disappears.
The next night
Its back again
And keeps returning
Its way- in light
Thru the days.
And knows...
It can- in fun
While you chase
The moon, to catch
And run…by,
Chasing,chasing the moon-your way.

The Moon

You can holler
At the moon
And if you do
The moon will go away
A little bit every day.
But it'ul come back
Again, and stay
Like it was before
It'ul remember too...
But it don't care
But other folks might
If they see you
Holler at the moon
When the moon
Is bright.

Folks Do

What folks do sometime
Is hard to understand
The things they do
And why they do
The things they do
Why if they could see
The way others see
What in their minds
They do the things- they do
What we all do- at times
Why we would all be
Much more perhaps
Than we be...
What all we folks do- sometime
Is hard- very hard to understand.

Memory

I looked and looked
And looked for you
Then I remembered
You're always
In my memories
That's a wonderful
Most beautiful place
To remember and be
Staying
There...
There in memory
Stored in memory, my memory
I found you lovely as always
In memory.

Different

Now lizards
Don't ride skate boards
And I'm quite sure
If dinosaurs were here
They would not too.
Alligators can't say hello,
Ask the reindeer
If they do.
Elephants can`t dance
At least I've never
Seen them
Even try to.
And mosquitoes bite
Bees they sting
And fleas do
Tiny little things
To make you itch
Like everything.
We all are different
In many ways
And learn from
What we do
That makes you- you
Me me
The lizards, lizards
And all others
Who they are too.
Now isn't that nice
Just like the white
On rice.

Our way

Tho she is gone forever
Forever gone away
In yonder cemetery
Put there soon- 2 years ago
To stay
We have our conversations
Some may not think
Tis- so
But we understand
At least I do
In our own special way
She speaks as if before
Almost as much of old
To me its so- and of
The old.
Means much in silence
And fills the space
Special... she filled for
Nearly 60 years, before
She left- to forever stay
Tho she is gone forever
We now have conversations
At least for now. Sometime
Our way.
Our silent way.

Sure Nice

Its a nice day
Its a sunny day
No clouds in the
Sky- I can see
Right now
For the sky is blue
Blue skies are nice
Too.
Today's
Sure nice,
Just passing thru.
And...
If you were here
I think you
Would
Think so too

Doves

Two doves just landed
Here together they flew
As they came by
And together they stay
They must know
Each other.
As least it seems so
Today
Two doves
The two doves
That flew here
So quiet...
As they came today
It seems...
Doves speak- doves way- silently.

Men

Greed greed
When it sows its seed
Men men
When they pick it up
Most times-do indeed
do strange things that,
They're sorry for.
Almost sometime
Even- go to war.
Greed greed
When it sows its seed
Men men
When they pick it up
Like it or not-
Do strange things
Not soon forgot.

Today

Children are playing
Out side today
The sun is shining
The sky is blue
Blue very blue today
Some birds are flying
But not too many.
I wonder where
The rest of the birds
Are today.
There must be many
Oh.
Maybe they are flying
In the sunshine
The sunshine is so bright
And makes just lovely
Light every where today
That's why the children
Are playing
Are playing out side
The sky is blue
The sun is shining
Some birds are flying
Everything is quiet
And nice
Its just a most lovely
Just beautiful,
Day.
Today.

It's Cool

The wind is blowing
It´s cloudy too
The sun is shining
It´s cool today.
Maybe...
The wind is,
Blowing
The warm away.
It´s cool today
It´s really,
Cool today.

The Tennis Court

We went to the tennis court
Today so the children
Could run and play
The tennis court
Is long and wide
And wide and long
All painted green
With great white stripes
In shapes of square
And nets of many stretched
Tight real tight
Between posts- with hardly room
To stretch them more.
The children love the tennis court
They bounce basket balls
They run and play
And play and run
Have great, great fun
In the sunshine
A sky of blue
Very, very blue
All day right thru
At the tennis court
Thats what it was
Today
When we went to the
Tennis court
With the children
Had great great fun
Today.

For Free

The rat race
The rat race
Many speak of
Take time- take time
Take time- to get away from
To get away from
Out of the rat race
Of life for a while
As time goes by
And year's go by.
It would be nice at times
As age creeps
Makes years slip by.
But... to even have a
Rat race
From which- to take
Excess time
Which comes to all
Even you and me- with age
For absolutely
Free.
Is difficult.

Ears

When it´s, really-really
Quiet
Your ears they
Listen, listen, listen
For any noise
They can hear.
Those ears...
They like to hear
Hear
Hear
Hear
Those ears
They like to hear.

Smiled

A child
Passed me by today
And smiled
Said hi
In a happy way
It´s nice
To see a smile
Hear hi
Most any time
Any day
It makes a better
Night
Or
Day.

To Say

If you say yes
And they say no
And others hear
And think
No should be yes
They may vote
Then to change no
To be, a yes.
But,
It takes-one person
To say
A yes or no
To make
It-so.

A Tall Tree

If you pass by
A tall tree
With green leaves
And there is
A blue sky.
Look thru
The tree limbs
Green leaves
At the sky
Its nice to see
And soft to the eye.
Try it, sometime
If you pass by
A tall tree
With green leaves
And there is
A blue sky too,
As you pass,
Thru.

One's Body

To walk or to run
Or
To sit and to stare
And
To think how to do
What's
To do over there
One...
Must get up
From
The soft easy
Sofa or chair
And get
Ones body
Right over there
And do
What's to do
Done...
Over there.

Hair

What hair I had
They took it back
And never sent
It back to me.
Now I don't
Have much on the top
Haven't had much there
Since they
Took it back.
When I was in my
Six-tees

Tub

There's roley poleys "(in dirt)"
In that tub
A lot of them
In there too.
They are crawling
Around, around, and around
Up the sides
And down the sides
Around, in the bottton too
They don't know
What to do
They are going
Here and there
But still
Are in there.
If they had wings
I'm sure
They would fly away
And never ever
Come back this way again,
To that old
Roley poley tub,
But...
They might like it
In there too
I don't know how to ask them
Do you?

96

About Bees

I seen them
Coming this way
A big swarm
Of them too.
I thought that they
Might stay,
But then they
Went away,
About bees,
You never know
Just what-they may do
And...
I seen them
Coming too.

A Gossip

Just listen
To the mocking bird
Carefully
And you can hear
What the
Mocking bird
Hears.
Because
The mocking bird
Likes to
Tell every body,
Most everything...
The mocking bird
Hears.
A gossip, a gossip
The mocking bird
The mocking bird
Tells, what
It hears

A Reason

Christmas season
Brings a reason
To wonder-children and all
At the snow
To wonder
At no snow
To wonder
At the sunshine
And where-just where
Did thanks giving go
And a reason
For some
To be sad.
A reason
For Christmas tinsel
Santa Claus
Happy songs
A babe born in a manger
No room in the inn
Of shepherds in snow
Of cows in a stable
Christmas season
And a reason
Of wise men too-following
A star of bright
To
The eternal birth of a
Holy child
And Christmas season
Light
Christmas gives a reason
To the season.

.

A Nice Thing

Holding hands
Is
A nice thing
To do
It gives
A feeling of
Very nice.
From you to me
And...
Me to you
And-others
Holding hands
With us,
Too.

The Sky

When the noon time, sun
Drops low in the sky,
And the color of
Purple come
Starting here, there
Far near, soon every where
All over, to the eye-and
Evening hours
Are night
Soon night creeps in
With stars and
Mystery of moonlight,
Star light, light with
And certain love, to the sky-this time starts,
when noon time sun
Starts to drop low...
In the sky.

Spring Time

Oh see all the small
New blossoms-on trees
Its spring time
Its spring time
Soon leaves on trees
Will come, to see
And soft breezes too
Will be passing thru
To rustle leaves
On trees
Birds will come
Make nests in the trees
And raise their families
All the birds will sing
Sing lovely songs, in the trees
Oh see the leaves
On the trees
Move in spring breeze
And birds sing too
Its spring time
Its spring time
For you and, me too.

Sun

As the-sun moves
and the shade
moves
. shadows
Get longer still
Till
Twilight comes.
Then shade
and shadows
are still.
And...
Become one.

It Flew

I seen an airplane
Flying by
And it flew
And it flew
And it flew
It flew
As I watched
It fly
Right into
The blue
Of the sky.

Thru Love

As the snow flakes
Fall to earth
Falling soft-like falling rain
No two snow flakes
Are the same
Quite a like, all are
Each one tho, not quite
All the same-but fall with a love
Tho no one the same, in design.
But we all thru love
Can give thru love
Tho each person not the same
For true love comes
From the inner heart
Right thru.
And glows like sunshine
From above,
With light to all
As eternal love.
Like the snow flakes
That fall
Soft, soft with a love
To and for the earth.

Childhood

With,
Water paints-water cans,
Water tables-jungle gyms
Tricycles, toys muddy places
Fun things to do
That's the place
Where small children like to go
Have lots and lots
Of fun there too
Getting wet
Children's style
With their friends
Together
Learning, playing
While they
With all the fun
Things to do
Quietly pass...
Childhood
Thru.

Seen

Thru my Window
I just seen
A little boy
Run past my house
"Oh"there he
Goes back too.
Doing what only
A child can do.
Thru my Window
I just seen,
Child hood...
Youth, passing thru.

The Sands-The Ocean

One day the
Drifting, shifting, loose
Solid, sinking, swallowing
Tide moving sands
Of the shores, of the ocean
And its friend the ocean
Invited me-to,
Go and explore
The shores of the far-far away-with
The vessels, its friend, the ocean, and all
it carries nights and days
To the shores of the
Far, far away
And see the world
That it sees, and the
Seas and the oceans, the people,
And the shores of different lands
Thru the days, and days today's
And years and days.
And I accepted-traveling
Thru today's and days
Thru years and days.
Enjoying, returning
Thanking, the drifting, shifting,
Solid, sinking, swallowing
Tide moving sands
Of the ocean
And the ocean
As they tirelessly move
Day by day
Speaking to all
In-its,
Mild thunderous
Addictive way.
To the adventurous, spirit
Of others.
Thru adventures...
Of
The far-far
Far away.

Forever

When you left
So quiet too
I had dozed
For a few moments
On the sofa
Right near you
You were with me
And everyone when
I lay down,
But maybe for 10 minutes
Later when I returned
You had left very
Quietly gone
Had soft closed the door
And went I never forget
That night, that day
Forever in my memory
It will stay.
For I was near you
Only 4 or 5 feet away
When you left forever
The evening of that day
I was near, that April 15,2010
Our 58 years
All thru together
And together we will
Always be.
Tho you left
So quietly too
You were called
Eternally and...
With love
But...
In my memory you will always be
The lovely wife, mother and
Everything true love could give
To me
Your husband.
With love.

It Seems

The body while living
It here can stay
The corpse must soon
Be put away
Its cremated- becomes
Ashes tho...
They here can stay
It seems
When life´s living
Magic
Slips away
Only memories
Remain, lengthy
All other
Is eternally
Thru,
And
Put away.

Nothing

The nothing tree
The nothing tree
Everything is free
On the nothing tree
Where oh where
Is the nothing tree
It´s right over there
The nothing tree
There´s nothing over there
I´m looking over there
Why...
You´re looking at nothing
That´s the nothing tree
Nothing tree
Nothing tree
You see nothing-you get nothing
That´s the nothing tree
Nothing is for free
That´s...
The nothing tree.

Most

Of the corpse-there is
Apprehension, of the ashes-all is ok
Of the living-there is fear
Why does
This exist, why is this
Feeling here?
Why oh why-is this belief
So close, to most who apprehend
And fear-the unknown?
Or, that of the little-of it
To them,
That is known.

Rains

If it rains today
The rabbits
Get wet
The squirrels
The mice
Get wet
Too.
But, the turtles
Dont care
If it rains today
They take their
House along
They´ll be ok.
They might
Even
Sing a song
A happy
Turtle song...
In the rain,
If-it
Rains
Today.

The Day

In my rocking chair
At the end
Of the end
Of the day
I rock
The cares
Of the
Contacted world
Away.
And I´m free
To sleep, in bed
From night-till day.
My rocking chair
Helps...
At the end
Of the day.
In.its
Special-relaxing,
Way.

My Playhouse

In my play house
There are no windows
Or even doors
We lay on the floor.
My friends can come
My friends can go
Any time they want
To come or go
My play house is nice
As we want, it to be
It would be nice
To have
A top, windows
And doors
But the pillows
Are soft as they
Can be
And we pretend
There's windows
And doors
To see
My play house is nice
Really really nice
As we want
It, to be.

Thought

Lost and lonesome
Is one-
Or two, almost-same, thought's-
And a good thought
Can bring either thru
To start again
From...
Lonesome again
From...
Lost again-is,
To...
Start, over
Again.

102

Rain Today

The clouds they are
So dark today
It looks like it
Might rain today
And a little
Rain
Fell down
Its kind of cold
Today
The clouds are
Still, so dark
It looks-like it
Might...
Rain today.
Seems like
The weather
It don't know
What to do.
And its trying, trying
Hard
Very hard.
To something,
Do.

Some Where

The wind is blowing here
The wind is blowing there
The wind is blowing every where
The wind is blowing birds
Flying high
The wind is blowing
Clouds, in the sky
The wind-the Wind
We can not see
Because the wind, it hides
From you-and me
But...
The wind is always blowing
Blowing somewhere-its way
Every where
Every day.

Let Me Know

Its raining today
And...
The grass is getting wet
The trees are getting wet
The birds are getting wet
The flowers are getting wet
The animals are getting wet
Do you think the
Clouds
The moon and stars
Are too?
If you know
Please let me know
Because,
When the rain
Comes thru.
I'd like to know
What the rains
Up to.

The Rain

Today in the rain
I see
A bird flying
A leaf falling down
Leaves moving on a tree
The wind is blowing too
I can not see the wind
Can you see the wind
As the wind blows today?
Out in the rain
A bird is wet
The leaves are wet
Do you think the wind
Gets wet
In the rain today
Too?
As the wind blows,
Who-oo-oo-who-oo-oo,
Thru.

Don't Know

Out side inside
Out side inside
Out sides cold
Out side inside
Insides warm
Out side inside
Lets stay warm
Out side inside
Out side inside
Out side nice
Out side inside
Lets stay nice
Out side inside
Out side inside
What will you do?
We don't know now, we're children-
Tell you when...
We're thru.

A Plant

I see a plant
With purple flowers
The plant has green leaves too
Together...
They make,
A pretty flower
I guess that's
What flowers do.
And
I really like
That plant
With purple flowers,
Its real real
Pretty,
Flowery purple
Too.

3 or 4 or 5 or 6 or 50

It's so much fun
When
You are 3 or 4 or 5 or 6 or 50
To pour water
On the sand-to
Make a puddle
That will grow
And grow
To make a good big
Old muddy real
Squishy, squishy, squishy
Mud puddle
Where you can
Just jump up
And down
Splash mud-every where
And, all around.
That's really, really fun
Real great big fun
When you are
3 or 4 or 5 or 6 or 50
Just to make this
Big, big
Squishy-squishy-squishy
Watery-mud puddle
Jump up,and down
And splash mud
Just about every where
And all around
Get your clothes
All dirty too.
That's a fun fun
Thing to do.
When you are
3 or 4 or 5 or 6
or 50.
Just try it sometime-I dare you.
Especially-if, you're 50.

Came By

Tonight my friend
Came by
I cooked a meal
And we ate
Finished and talked
For hours
Just reminiscing.
Both had recently
Lost our wives
Of nearly 60 years
But we had
A very nice time
Expanding-depleting
Building-diminishing
Remembering
The years-and memories
With love
In silence
Sadness, too
Tonight.
When my friend
Came by.
We too...
Went back
Said hi-our way.

Egg

He said
He just found
A dinosaur egg
And said it was
From a T...rex too.
Not many,
Of that kind
And...
When you´re only
4 years old,
They are especially...
Hard to find.

Dreams

Meadows exist
Where there are lovely
Valleys, of verdant green
And where there are
In the heart
Deep depths to
Fertile dreams connecting
To tides-that,
We ride
As clouds,
Drifting on high
To other places
Of love
Where verdant
Valleys and meadows
With flowers and
Beauty and
The lovely-say,
Hi...at times in dreams.

Will Be

On your leaving
Never to return
Was a part of life
I never wanted
Life
To turn, that way
To be.
Tho...our turn
Must come-must be.
Yet-your leaving
Never to return
Is a part of me
I´ll always remember
With love
A part of life
My life
It will be
Always-always
Be.

Some How

Right now
At pictures
Im...
Looking, looking, looking
Traveling, traveling, traveling
From there
To here
From here
To there
To
Some where
Quietly.
Right now... in memories
Looking, looking, looking
Thinking, thinking, thinking
Traveling, traveling, traveling
Some how
And
Wow...
Right now-wow, wow-those,
Pictures have a way of speaking
Yet we never hear a word.

Bye

A child
A
Rock
Let
Fly-at
The
Glass
A
Window, window-
Bye
Bye.

Fronds

Leaves of palm trees
Fronds of palms
Waving in the wind I see
Neath a blue sky
Blowing free
And the leaves of
Palms neath
The sky of blue I see
Make a beautiful
Picture
Just for me
Neath a sky-so blue
To see
Leaves of palm trees
Fronds of palms
In the wind
And...
Blowing free.

Pretty

A maple tree-with leaves
Of the colors
Red and mixed
With green
As the tree does
Grow and grow
Must know,
It is pretty, very pretty
When it is seen
With its leaves
Of red and mixed
With green
For sometime
Tho they are usually
Very very still
Sometime
The leaves will flutter
With a nearly silent
Breeze
Saying thank you
For noticing, viewing me
While
Passing thru.

Pretend

Little girls
In their pretend
Beauty shop
Fixing hair
In their shop
Their way.
Paying how much
Their charge
And such
For their beauty work
In their shop
With play money
Their way
This I watched today
Near their shop
Little girls-mostly girls
Sometime boys
Curious boys
In the busy
Busy beauty shop
Of pretend…
Toy lands,
Way
Today.

Light

To see the light
Of day
To be of
The light of day
In beautiful ways
Thru hope care
Love and trust
In all creation
Is beautiful lovely-and is
A gift-a gift
Of love
Gods love
Eternal love
To see the light
To be of
The light of day.

Today

Its supposed to rain
Its supposed to rain
Its supposed to rain
At 4 o' clock today.
And...
If it don´t rain
At 4 o' clock
It will be
A very nice day
today
But if it rains
At 4 o' clock
Like its supposed
To rain today
It will be
A
Rainy day
A rainy day
And I want sunshine
At 4 o' clock,
Today.

Their Way

So many birds-are in the sky
Flying so high-and really close by
Not saying a word-as they go by
Where are they going
Not known to you
Not known to me
Only the birds know
Only the birds
So many birds in the sky today
Flying high, happy
And flying their way
So many birds-so many birds
Traveling...
Traveling, traveling their way-up
Way up in the sky.

Can-Not

I can see the back
Of you
And you cannot
You can see the back
Of me
And I cannot
I can see the front
Of you
And you can see the front
Of me
And together we can see
The front of us
The back of us
And others too.
While together we can
See...
Much and too much
Of others.
As they pass, on their way thru.
Where I can see
The back of you
And you can not
And...
You can see the back
Of me
And I cannot
Others that we pass
They to-cannot
Perhaps they really

Don't care
This...know we?
We do not.
But...
This one thing
We cannot do
Of this-one thing
We know
Tis true
That...
You can see
The back of me
And I cannot
And... I
The back of you
And...
You
Cannot.

continued

108

A Heart

To draw...
The shape of a heart
Is so different to see
Its never the same
For you-as for me
It might not-be as big
It might not be
As small
It might to me-in shape
Look ok
To you, it might
Look
In shape-for you
As not-ok
The shape of a heart
To be
Is so different to see
Its never, quite the same
Even,
A real heart...
In feeling
Or shape
For you...as for me.

Little Bird

One day
A little bird
Flew
To a little tree
With green leaves
By my window
Turned its head
A funny way
And sat
Looking at me
Thru my window
A bird and me
Looking, looking
Staring, strangely
At each other
Thru a window
Then...
The little bird
All finished
I assume...
Flew away.
They have, to- birds do.

Every Day

The sun is free
The clouds are free
The stars are free
The moon is free
The rain is free
The snow is free
Isn't it
Just lovely
And
Beautiful
So much is free
To enjoy
Every day...
For every body.

The Hill

Up the hill
Down the hill
Around the hill
Over the hill
Faster slow
Any way you want to go
The hill-the hill
Will wait
For you.

Wagons

There's wooden wagons
Metal wagons
Plastic wagons too
That children play with
When they play
And play thats what they do.
The metal wagons
Wooden wagons
Most they seem to stay
The plastic wagons
Seem to break
And soon they fade away
The wooden wagons
Metal wagons
These one cannot find
There's only plastic
Wagons
They're welcome too
If they'd stay here
But they fade away,
And soon– they're thru.

Interest

Kind of lost interest
In a whole lot of things
Don't really know
Why this is so
Cause if the sun
Went down-at noon
I'd be peeved, and would feel-bad
maybe rest of the day that
I'd been, deceived.
Or if it rained and rained
For a month and a day
Now that really, really, really
Would not be ok.
But I guess I really
Lost interest
In things that are ok
And my interest will come back
Tomorrow, today
Maybe before-and,
That's ok.

A Pig

There's a pig in the sky
There it is flying by
See its head, see its tail
In the sky?
No, that's a cloud
You only think
Its a pig.
Well, it looked like a pig
Maybe it was a pig.
But pigs don't fly.
Maybe sky pigs do
Like clouds drift by
Sky pigs fly-and elephants too,
Way, up in the sky-but,
Only...
When you want them,
To.

A Hug

A good honest hug
Gives good warm
Comforting feelings
All the way thru
From head
To your feet
And
Around you.
Then goes on
Its way
To make a nice day
With many good feelings,
Starting...
With-and from
Just, hugs.

110

Spring

Spring is shouting
The leaves are out
The leaves
And all, are green
The grass is green
And birds are singing
Making nests
And sitting
In the trees
Frogs are croaking
Bees are here
And fish are
Jumping too
The snow is
Gone from
All around
Its spring time
Its spring time
The flowers know it
The blossoms know it
Grasshoppers know
And crickets too
Spring is shouting
Spring is shouting
Its spring, its spring
I'm passing thru
I'm here for you.

Done

Number one
If you don't know
It can't be done
You may do it
And its done.
Number two
If you know
It can be done
You never try
You never get thru.
Just how its done
When its all thru.
Its up to you.

Forgotten

Something good
Thought forgotten
This is not so
For it has changed
You
In its way
Before it left
To go.
And will be there
When called on
With something good
Thru you
To do so.

Close

The sky is seen
As heavenly blue
But sometime its
Some cloudy too
Tho up above
The clouds so high
And even in
The darkest night
A heavenly blue
Is close, tho high
If seen as
Heavenly, heavenly
Sky
Is always blue
And heavenly nigh.
Also
Creators love
A heavenly
Blue of sky
Thru faith
For all. to all
Is always
Close
Always
Nigh.

Thru

Where the sleeping sleep
Be quiet, be quiet
Be quiet as can be.
For there sleep
Is what to do.
For all who passeth thru
Where sleep is all
The sleeping do.
There is no other task,
To do.
And when one enters
The world of sleep,
Professional sleepers
all, become.
Other works all finished
Done.
For there sleep
Is what to do.
For all...
Who passeth thru.

A Fun Thing

Running and holding
This paper too
You holding the paper
And me too.
We both can run
Just as fast-as we can
The paper-just flutters
And blows when we do-in the wind,
Its really-its really
A fun thing to do.
Running and holding
Some paper too-lets call it a kite
Yes-
Lets call it a kite.

Stepping

Walking, walking
Stepping anew
To a place we all
Never before know-may call,
On the king of creation
the leader
Of all
Whom answers
If we in true faith
Do call.
To direct
Our steps
As we walk
And we wish
With love
On the creator
To call.
As we are walking, walking
Stepping a new
On paths we have
Never been
Or-knew
When...
Walking-walking
Stepping anew
The creator-always listens
Directs
With love.

Vulture

Vulture-vulture
One I see
Flying by that
Big old tree.
Where's he going
This I know
To find something
On the ground be low.
Vulture, vulture
One I see
I see you...
But you don't see me.

Best

I want to say something
I want to do something
I don't know what to do
So I guess-I'll go
Help some body
Or do something-good to do
I guess its best
To do that
And say something good
Then
Too.

4 Crows

4 crows flying
In the sky
4 crows flying
Right close by
1 crow just flew away
3 crows flying
In the sky
3 crows flying
Right close by
1 crow just flew away
2 crows flying in the sky
2 crows flying right close by
1 crow just flew away
1 crow flying right close by
That crow just flew away
No more crows in the sky
I see
No more crows flying
Close by me.

Slid

I got angry at the world
The world didn't care
It seemed to choose
And tell me-hey you...
Go find joy some where
We the world are to big
To worry about just one
There's many many
In this world and
You are but one
And there's much, much
Good-bad, happy, joy
To be found. Go...
Make the right choice
That's what you must do
Don't be angry with me
The world look inside
Too...with you
And I did,and...
Slid thru-the world...
Went along too.

There Be

Just imagine
From sea to sea
What folks do
And...
How they be
The good-the bad
And mediocre too
The days-the nights
Summers, winters, seasons lives
As they come
As they come
As they go
Much passes thru
And everyday too
Just imagine
From sea to sea
What really, really
All...
There be.

When

When someone
You love leaves
Never to come back,
Seems like something
Inside snaps.
And takes a long time
To go together-and back,
You get to almost the same.
But never, quite the same.
When someone you love
Leaves,
Never to again,
Come-back.

That Way

Sometime...
When there's lots to see
You don't see anything.
And-sometime
When there's nothing to see
You see just everything.
Why is this so?
I guess its so
Cause it must be,
That way...
Sometime

The Ball

If when riding
On a great large ball
You should accidently fall.
Get back on
And ride real soon
So you can better, with
Less fear, ride...
On the ball,
Again.

.

Learning

Tho
The school years
Almost finished
And
School's almost out
Learning
Never finishes
We learn something
Every day
We're in out
And about.
Freely-silently
Good and bad, we
Learn some everyday.
Tho
The school years
Almost finished
Schools almost out,
Learning-never finishes
It stays...
Round-about.

Gingerbread

Ginger
Is good
You can eat it too
Ginger bread
People
Look like people do
Ginger bread
Cookies-now
They're good too
Ginger bread
Crayon folks
I seen em
They're here...
Maybe sometime
You can see
Em
Too.
And when you do
They will
Look like, ginger bread
Folks
To you.

Do

When needed
Honestly needed
Do,
As much-as you can
If not
Call or make contact
As much-as you can
That way-after...
You will honestly know
You have done
As much-as you
Could do, when
You, were
Honestly
Needed.

Times

Sometime ones world
Is small
Only room
For one and
No more.
During those times
Only one
Should enter
Not
One-two-three
Four
Or more.

14 Months

It´s been almost 14 month´s
Since you left
I feel at times quite
Lonesome
Other times almost
But not fully ok
Never completely.
The same-as when
As before you left,
And when you were here.
In my mind that time
Will never ever come again.
I want it to tho,
I look for you
And,
You are here
And speak with me
In my mind-where you,
Stay with me
Tho...
Its been almost
14 months now
Since you left
The months always
Come and go
And the feelings do to
As the wind
Cycles as the seasons
Go.
And all from the creator
With love,
That I can feel
Around me always.
And when I view
Drifting clouds of white
Moving neath a sky of blue,
I think of-the creator
And you-and love
That always flows-flows,
More lovely...flowing thru.

Loves There

Hop scotch-is a game
That children play
As they grow, as they grow
Their childhood way
And
They mingle with others
Grow with others
Mix with others
In their way-study with others
Various studies
as they grow
traveling on-and thru
lifes road
and, all the way
meeting love-greeting love
children, others
thru
faith-families
too
even, as comes
understanding-misunderstanding
light, dark
lightning-thunder
rainbows
crying, flowers
also-leaving
loves there-all the way thru
quite...
like hop scotch is
a game
children play-adults too
their way, their choice
in life
as they grow-as we grow
with the creators love
always, there sustaining
as we grow.

Awake

To awake the old
And enliven the new
Remember a song
The words-of a
Long past-good times
Old favorite tune
Take a trip down
Memory lane.
Back to now
Awaken the old
Enliven the new.
Its good to do
Really economical
Too.

The Building

Hit the building
With a crane
Knock the building down
Break it up in pieces
Put and piled all around
Put the pieces
In a dumpster
Take the building
Out of town.
Throw the pieces
All away
No more building
Here today.
Now...
Take the crane
That hit the building
Take it
Far,
Fa-r-r-r away.

Break of Day

Its early in the morning
And here I am
Just readin and writin
And passing the time away
Early in the morning
And right before
Break of day
Seems like that's a nice
Time for me sometime
To go deep inside
Be just me-look at me
At others too.
And to me-to me, just be kind.
When its early-in the mornin
By...being me,
Just readin and writin
An passin the time, away.
Right before
Break of day.

A Seagull

Oh there comes a seagull
In for a landing right near
With both wings spread out
Not moving about
Lower and lower
The seagull glides
On air currents
Grace fully, grace fully glides
To a silent, sweet
Two point beautiful landing
Both feet on the ground
Just walking slowly
Looking around.

Painting

Many children-I see
Painting with water
And brushes
On pieces of wood
Having fun, fun, fun
Laughing, talking, everyone
Doing what others
Maybe...
Wish they could
Do,
Sometime.

A-Song

To be...
Right or wrong
Can be
As a song
That song alone
And I will sing
With you
Then together
We can find
The right or wrong
In our song, together
To be, and...
What it-may be.

Of True

To tell-of true
Tell
Tell
Tell
If they
Don´t believe
You
Tell others-some never believe,
And
Tell tell
Tell
If you´re speaking-at times you must do,
To tell of true.

Storm

The rain before
After and during the storm
Is much the same.
Only before maybe
Slight and increase
In intensity to
Become just right
To blow with wind
To grow to a storm
Of great
Or little
And gentle
In beauty and love
With
A rain bow-that comes
In silence-quiet, after the storm
Spreading comfort memory
Lovely
For all...
After the storm.

Shadows

A shadow comes
In light with me
And stays with me
For all to see
Because...
Shadows like the light
Like me.
Your shadow is
In dark there too
And if a light-just...
Shines on you
You can see it too
Because...
Shadows like the light-must have light-just,
like you.

As You Are

Just come as
You are
That's the way
That it has to be
You are the one
That's called
To be seen
The one that's called
To see whom
You be
Or have been
Just come as you are
For...
That's who you
Really, really
Are.

Sand

I love the beach
I love the sand
I love to walk
At beach
In the
Sandy-sandy
Dry, wet, loose
Rolling, fun
Hard, easy
To walk in
Sandy-sandy
I just love to
Walk at the beach
In the sand.

Then

Smaller and smaller
To be
With fewer-and fewer
Of things-to do
Soon, soon
With nothing
Nothing to do.
Then...
Smaller-smaller
More small
And...
Nothing.

Balloons

Two balloons
Tied to a string
On a pole
Two balloons
Flying in the wind
Two balloons
Both of green
I seen.
Both in the air
Flying there
Oh yes,
And by the way
Those two
They are a pair...
Any time-any day
You may pass thru
And,
See them there,
Those-two balloons-flying,
Cause-
They're a pair.

The Best

Do the very best
You can do, all
The time
Is always right
To do
The best you can do.
So always
Do the very best
You can do-all the time.

Same

More, more, more
All is same
So more more.
No...no more
Are you sure?
Yes-more, more- I need more
You´ll be sorry
That´s ok-?
More, more, more
Stop, stop, stop
The handle broke
I told you-no more.
Oops...
That's for sure-
Now, not the same.

Rocks

One
Bucket
Two
Buckets
Three
Buckets
Four
I´m putting rocks
In the buckets
But I need
Some more.
Rocks more rocks
Oh where
Can they be?
Hey...
They´re right over there
Look...
Can´t you see?

Inside

You have to go inside
Deep inside
Work with your self
Inside-be honest
Come to grips fully
With you
Work the problem
Out
Smooth the problem out
Completely
Honestly
With you.
And get on with life.
First tho...
You have to go inside
Where the heart
Is.
To-start, really start.

Essential

Showers and bath´s
They are essential
And yes,
We need then too
Just like
The rooster
When he crows
He has to
Do that too
Cock-a doodle
Oh yes...
And doodle
doodle-do.

Stay

What the years
Have done
Can never be changed
Completely...
In any way
For something will stay
For the future
To see
For what the years
Have done
Something was left
The years way...
To
Always
Stay.

Whoosh

The year´s
They don´t say
Anything
Any whoosh
They´re gone
They´re thru
They leave much
Of something
Or nothing-of something
For every one
But everyone can see
The way
They handled you
And the way
You handled-them too.

Bye

A child
A
Window
A
Rock
Let-fly
The glass
Of
A-window-it hit, window...Bye, bye.

Afternoon

Sunshine too
With a sky of blue
And a little breeze
Softly blowing thru
Makes an afternoon
That really-pleases you.

Everything

Sometime
The old of things
Come thru to me
The new of things
And-I compare them to
The now of things-they come quite differently
How things, they were
In the many many
Months-years before
That can never
ever be
For progress must be
For all humanity
To move-on and on
And on.
But some hour...
I like to recall
The old of things
And then compare
The old and new
Together
Then
That gives me the best.
Of everything.
Sometime

To You

Change your stockings
Every day
This with your shoes
Do too.
If this you do
You
Your feet-and others too
May silently
Like...what,
You did, to you.

The Winds

The winds-blew and blew
And caused a new
A kind of change
In me and you
As we passed by.
Gently casting, an eye
On the silent moving
Shadow-of a bird
In the sky
Of its shadow cast-
On the counter top,
From the winds of life
That never stop.
As they in silence
Blew and blew-the bird passing
Passing
Just...passing thru.
As we passed the counter top
On a cabinet of life.
As life's winds, softly gently blew.

Ways

The quiet-the noise
A silence too
And thunder
Then lightning
A rainbow shining
Thru...
On clouds
is beautiful
Bringing
Quiet, noise
Thru silence
To some
In
Many ways.

Get Lost

To get lost-in you
Is hard to do
But is not hard when,
you try a little too
Just write about
The things you do,
Have done, the good,
The bad and other too
You want to
You´ll be surprised
Its not hard.
To get lost-in you
But...
Do it in a good way
Tho
Too.

Strange

Hey...
Who´s that new
Strange person?
Why that´s you,
You don´t know you?
No...but thank you
Because
You can see,
The strange new me
Who I don't see
But now I see
The person who
Was strange
To me.

Sound

The sound of an engine
I hear in the sky
And its not the
Choppity chop of a helicopter
Flying by-its not
A car, or a truck,or a bus
Or a ship-because...
They don´t fly
Oh, its only an airplane
And the propeller
Said hi
And that's
I, the airplane
High in the sky
Listen-listen
I...am passing by.

Soft Music

A sky of haze
Warm lazy
Sunday afternoon
Eatin a crunchy.
Tostada
And a big burrito
Too.
An doin just nothin
Is a,
Very nice
Way
To-pass
The afternoon
Thru.

Day by Day

Birds fly in the sky
Have since creation began
Contribute much to the earth
In a beautiful way
Day by given day.
Airplanes they to
Fly high in the sky
Sharing with birds
The spacious
Of heavenly sky
And changing the earth
Have since their birth.
While the sky-maybe watches
With wonder-in its way
Birds, man, and...
Civilizations changes
Marvelous, mysterious changes
Day by day.

Who

Who are you?
Are you the you
You think you are?
If you we tested
For the 100% you
Would you honestly
Still be you
If not
Who are you?

The Twilight

A bird-a robin
During twilight hours
Landed
Quiet, oh so quiet
On my lawn
In the twilight
Looked this way-that way
Then...
Quiet, oh so quiet
As I looked, too,
And quick.
The robin...
Was up-in the twilight
And...just,
Flew away.

Over

High over the clouds
Where the sky is blue
And much higher still
The stars, the moon
And the sun-live too
Right under all this
Folks on an airplane-can
Fly by
Most times we never
Know why.
But maybe...
The sun, the moon
The stars
The deep blue sky
Know
They passed, by.

Some Time

Make noise
Make waves
Like
Thunder does-storms do
The wind does
When it goes thru
Flapping the flag
On the flag pole
On a windy day
The ocean also makes a roar
And airplanes
Make a noise
In the sky
When they go by
Same time-tho
Keep poise
But...
Sometime
Make noise.

There

I don´t know why
It came there
I guess it came
To stay
Because it never-ever,
It never...
Went away.
I don´t know why
It came
To stay.

Dreams

Isn´t it strange
What dreams
Can do?
The one you
Dream of
It seems
In dream´s way
Someway
Is right there
With you too.
And even
Sometime...
May-talk,
To you,
Isn´t it strange.?

A Dreamer

Just thinking, comprehending
Designing
Aware-unaware
Of surroundings
In a world
Of their own-is the dreamer
And being in
The world of...
A dreamer
Designing how
Something, seen-in the mind
Will be.
Later performing-assisting in
Producing, what he or she see´s.
Is how much of what,
We see-we use
Comes to be.
From the mysterious
Interesting world.
Of...
A dreamer.

A Burning Campfire

The flames of a burning campfire
As they light the dark of night.
Kind of weave
A little sunshine
With love,
Some how...
In the night.

The Call of the Ocean

I love the roar of the ocean
As it calls thru the fog to me.
Its call has perhaps
Been the same.
For many and others, the same as for me.
But I love the roar of the ocean
And as the fog falls quietly.
I´ll listen to the call of the ocean
And hear centuries-calling,
Just...calling to me.

On and On

Ocean mist
Upon the face
Strikes lightly
Then its gone
The
Ocean´s roar
Continues on
For centuries
On and on.

Lights

Lights in the fog
Are shrouded it seems
And lights
In the clear
Are clean
Like in a dream.

A Bee– A Fly

There goes a bee
Just flying by
A bee´s a bee
And not a fly
A bee can sting
But not a fly.
Don´t get a bee
Mixed with a fly.
If you do
You´ll know quick, why.

Guiding

Stars are beautiful
They light up the sky
With a soft
Glowing light
Guiding-from
Heaven high.

Ciders Warm

Crisp the air
The ciders warm
Sky of blue
In early morn
Frosty air
And breaths you see
Decorations
Christmas trees
Children-old folks
All you see
Happy-lonesome
Left to be.
Crispy air
The ciders warm
Inside, thru faith
A love, is born.

Beauty

Large or small
No matter what
The beauty-of beauty
No matter large or small
Beauty to each
Comes from a need
To see beautiful
Large or small
In what we interpret
Beauty to be
From what
We be hold
Then
We touch-we feel
Imagine
Or,
We see, beauty.

Ancient Roar

The oceans roar
When its quiet and still
Is constant-unchanging
For ever near
And to the listening ear
Give´s
A lullaby
Of the past
And the when
With the now
And...
The near
In a
Soft-thunderous
Constant-ancient
Roar.

Seagulls

Three seagulls
In the sky
Three seagulls
Not too high
Three seagulls
Right close by
Three seagulls
Flew away
No more seagulls
Here today

Clouds

Thru tree leaves
Green- I see
A sky of blue
With clouds
Of white
Peeking down
At me
And an airplane
High
Up in the sky
Flying by
Is close
To the clouds
Of white
As they-drift by.

Shows

What you are thinking
Shows on your face
It shows like a map
All over the place.
Think of something happy
Maybe that will do
To help show some
Happy on your face
Maybe...
Make you more happy too.
Because
What you are thinking
Shows on your face
Shows like a map
All over the place.

Fault

Whose fault-who is to blame
For all to name
For where or
What to do, was done
Who seen or, had to do
With what-we heard
Or seen, pass thru
Was it of now-or of
The coming soon
That knows of
A problem here
And with us now
That gives discomfort
The discomfort
That occurred-all now can see.
Whose fault can this be?
Let this blame-come in honesty
As the sun, moon, we see.
The creation comes in honesty
So must the laws of blame then be
Then...whose fault this be
All will see
We must have, create and make
Our laws to be
With such great honesty
That we trust fully
Then we will know
Without a doubt-and who to blame
For this-and other troubles too
When they-pass thru.

Speak

For children
Speak up
Speak up
For
Children
For they
Can´t
Speak up
For
Them selves
So do
For
Children
Speak up.

Some Folks

Check the oil pressure, tachometer,
Fuel gauge too
Engine sounds ok-check outside fuselage ok too
About all you can do.
Much else, is
Out of your hands-fire er up-taxi, lift off
Then...
Look down at,
The disappearing land
Flying above
Most alone-high,
In the sky...
Still in the airplane.
Exciting, frightening
Loveable too
Kind of fuels
The human engine
In some folks
Too.

The Return

For one
To have returned
To the place, a sacred place
Where one-of ones love
Left from, when called
And left there
A trace of love
Is beautiful,
For that in turn
Welcomes, giving
The best-that deep
Inside always waits
With welcome feelings of love
At the return
Of that one...
With love, with song
With deep felt expression feels
At the sacred place
Silently-but complete
And...
Understood.
By the one that thru love
Returned.

A Year

Its been more than a year
Now since you left me
A year this April 15th
Since you went away
Now at times-I can hear your voice
Your words speaking-in your way
With guidance
To what I maybe thinking of
At the time guiding, speaking
In your way.
Others may think, this is not so
But for me, think-and it is so
And...I´m happy that
In your way tho
You´re been gone
For more that a year
This way you´re here with me
Tho silently, nearly everyday
I hope that in someway-you
Can understand me too
None can say you understand-a true of yes or no
But you and I know,
Our love...that it is true
And has been-always will be
A special way-for ever and ever
And...
For always.

Waves

The ocean waves
So quiet can be
And with moon light too
Speak romantically
But with earthquake
Stirred...
Become angry too
And can create
Tsunami great
With waves, of large
Destroying creations
Wondrous life-land
Then...
Become again,
The ocean waves
So quiet
As quiet-can be.
Speaking, romantically
The ocean-the ocean
The ocean
With waves,
Of mystery...
The ocean.

It's Way

Suffering
Has a way
That
Brings healing
In a way.
That remains...
It lessen's
There
To stay-the,
Suffering...
Brought-
Its way.

Of You

On leaving the house
To the garage
Thru the little door
When I leave that way
Every time-everyday
Your shoes-the ones
You very last wore
Are sitting-where
You left them
When and if I accidently
move them
I replace them every time.
When I leave the house
Thru that door
To the garage
I place-my house shoes
Near your shoes
Everyday every time.
It makes me feel something
Inside good when I do.
I think of you.

To Do

Do all as it is
To be done
For all has a way
A proper way
To accomplish its
Ut most
On the road
Of life.
In all we do-try to.
Follow the road
To best carry
The load
Written and tested
As the proper way
Each day.
To and for all
And do
As it is to be done.
That way
You can
Most times
Do wonders...
And the wonders
Surprise
Even you
To do,
Even
More.

The Earth

Man was created
To walk the earth
With no wings
As birds to fly.
Then came the day
Man with machine
As birds could fly.
But when man
Leaves earth
The feel is there
You must come back
For it is not for you
To soar and soar
In sky of blue,
You are man-not, bird
You cannot fly
While in the air
Man must stay
In machine
Man has not wings
Man cannot
Fly.
When once again
With machine
Man toucheth earth
From sky above
There comes a feeling
Quite as with mirth
And that of love
That of the earth
I am of man
I have no wings
As birds to fly
I love the earth
For here, I, am I.

Love

We speak of love
But what is love
Is it the same
For you-for me
Is it the same
For me-for you
This of course-we must think thru
Love is close-as hate in a way
Love is is close-as night and day
Meaning not the same to each its way
Yes is quite the same in its own way
Binding close and tightly too-if true
Much the same as quality glue.
A mothers love-a fathers love
A siblings love too
Is much same all life time thru
For the family and must be,
To see them thru
The parents love-the siblings love
If true-is there, the same, all life thru.
For this love is never done
Family love must have understanding
We speak of love-but what is love?
It seems invisible
Tho its there every where every day
Clearly visible to others
Yet plentiful for all.
When understood is lovely too
All the way thru.

Thru Creation

An earthquake is so terrible
In all that it can do
On the surface of the earth
And underwater too.
How it can tremendously
Shake the earth.
Its almost unbelievable-what it can do,
In just, a very few minutes
Of any given day.
And underwater in oceans,
Deep deep in the earth
Where a ring of fire, some places live
And plates of the earth possibly
Connected with volcanoes together in a way
When moved birth an earthquake
Large or small to be.
And also cause a tsunami
In the earth to move-so that
If a large tsunami occurs
A very devastating, almost unimaginable
Part of life can be made to move
By the swirling of the waters, of the ocean
Near the tsunami as the waters move rapidly
To and fro carrying moving life-destroying life,
And things of life with great force
As the waves of water build to tremendous
Size.
Going to and fro over the earth
Swirling, swirling forcefully, carrying
Things, just things of everything places
Waves of the ocean never ever really go.
Giving birth so all can see
How the tremendous powers
Of creation thru creation
Can really, really be
In a few moments, and do
Moving the earth in such a way
Anytime, any day
As it passes with great,
Devastation...
An earthquake-and tsunami
Passes-rapidly,slowly
Never, ever soon to be forgotten...
Thru.

All Alone

Alone, alone I feel all all alone sometime,
In a small boat alone-lonesome...
On the wide open sea
Near the center
With waves of huge
White with foam
The boat rides high
The boat rides low
Having no knowledge
Of a boat to guide
The boat, and the waves- I ride, just ride
On the open sea
With waves of huge I ride
I am all alone I feel-all all alone
But now...the creator has come-I feel
And is here with me
In the boat with me
Bringing a spiritual love
A spiritual calm.
Now the creator and I
Together we ride
Alone, alone, all all alone
In the small boat alone
Tho now with the creator here
To help guide
Over the wide open sea
we ride-we ride
together...and safely,
we ride.

The Sky

Up where the sky
Is blue to the eye
Where the ground
Is far down below
Where the mountains
Are far
And purple with haze
And the horizon
Stretched straight
Then, hi lo, its way
In the airplane
Where one can see
All this
And much much more
To view,
One can miss.
As one guides the airplane
With wings
On same plane
As the horizon for far away
With mountains
Of hi lo, their way
As seen from up
Where the sky
Is blue to the eye
And
Where the ground
Is far-far
Down below.
There comes a feeling of bliss
Of lonesome-and accomplishment too
In the all-that man
And machine
Has done-and...
Can do.

Explained Unexplained

To explain
The depths of the ocean
Or the height of the stars
Or the way the wind rushes
As it travels, a far
Or to explain
The way that a seed
Tho it be-oh so small
Can produce life
That is beautiful
And necessary
For all.
Would be
A momentous task
Similar to...
As mountains are tall
But to explain
The love of
One for another
Blossom´s
That as flowers
Full beautiful
In early spring
Is a task that flows
As is explained
Thru faith
And love spiritually
To you and I
Congratulations
On your marriage
And may the love
That created
The oceans, the winds
The flowers beautiful

And all
Remain forever
In your lives

continued

Blossoming faithfully
Spiritually
As the seasons
And flow
Explained-unexplained
Just lovely
Lovely lovely
On, on
Forever
And on.

You

Just who are you ?
Can you tell me
Who you are
Can you tell me
Just how far
That you have came
Since birth.
Can you tell me
What to do-or,
If I should be
Doing right
By doing, just as you.
For I would like to know
I´m a bit confused
And want someone
To follow, and chose you.
Please can you tell me
Just how far
That you have come
Since from now
Back to where
All have started from.
So I can follow you
Since its you I´ve chose
To follow thru.
Please can you tell me
Just who, are
You?

Pathways

The beauty of a flower
The petals of a rose
So fragile
Yet so sturdy
Where lovely fragrance flows.
And memories linger round that flower
In fact they grow with years.
As sun beams glow
As spiritual beliefs
In folks we know.
And may the fragrance of love
Drift thru to you
For love is of God
This is known to be true,
In your plans for now
And the future too-your pathway
For your guidance
You feel is from special love
As the beauty of a flower
From God above.
Who lights pathways unknown
For faith
Hope
And love,
God is love.

The Corner

At the corner of the fence
Where the green grass grows
In the shade of an old pine tree
And flowers grow there
The birds nest there
And lovers leave names
On the old pine tree
That grows there-thru the years
Quite free.
And the grass, and the flowers
And the love, and the hours
Live quiet, live lovely
At the corner of the fence
Where the green grass lives grows.
Mixed with time-growing quiet-quite free.

Ways

Once the genie is
Let out of the bottle
To solve the problems
We see.
The genie may not think
As you, as me
And its very hard-to put
The genie, back
In the bottle-for you for me
Once the genies out
Its hard to say
If good-or bad
Will be...
The genies ways.
Once the genies out
So be careful
With the genie.

Hurt

The tree was hurt
When the limb was cut
The bird was hurt
When a wing was struck
The boy was hurt
Just a tiny bit
When his bicycle broke.
Then a little duck
Walked by-with a tear in its eye
Saying, I hurt deep inside
Where no one can see
When it hurts but me
Oh, we can see said the tree
We can see said the bird
For your face tell´s us more
Than you think we have heard.
And we care-like the wind
That blows-where you go
That blows-where you are
That blows where you´re been
And because we can help
Like the sunshine does
Because it lights up the dark
Thats deep, deep inside
Lights up the hurt
That went there to hide
Then the birds and the tree
And the duck, and the boy
Said please-Mr sun
Give us light, to enjoy.

Dawn's Glow

From what I can see
From where I've been
From what I've been thru
From what I've been
Told and had to do
From what I see here
And may have to go back
To do.
Don't make any sense
To me at all
There seems no way
None that see my way
Or appears about
To help.
My self or others
Like me
Can't you folks see
Or are you blind
We forever have,
Been left behind
But by silence we hear
And we compare
The here-the there
The there-the here
And we know
What you don't know
What you can't feel
What in your minds you-
Don't even see
So...
From what I see
From what I've been thru
From where I've been
And had to do
Don't make any sense
Te me at all.
Please send sunshine
To the twilight
That missed dawns glow.
Below
Far below.

Of Lovely

Think of the blossom
The flower too.
Think of a seed, a
Sapling-a small
And large tree too.
Think of an egg
Small-medium
Large bird, too
Think of a cloud
A storm-a rain bow too.
Think of dawn sunlight
Happines, a beautiful
Day too,
Think of noon, twilight
Evening, moonlight
Stars just shinig
Thru.
Think of all this
With family, flowers
Sunshine, storms,
Rainbows twilights
Evenings.
Aged with lovely
And...
Of lovely memories too.
The beautiful the lovely
Is in silence
There-just...shining thru.

138

Dawn

Early in the morning
And the dawn is near
While dark is waiting
For sunlight to appear
Is a wonderful time
For quiet is there
The world still sleeps
Awaiting soon coming day
To appear.
While early in the morning
And dawn being near
Night owls can hover
And relish,
The quiet-the mysterious
Wonderful there.
Early in the morning
Waiting for sunlight...
To-appear.

The Way

Sometime the numbers
You count
Seem to come
When you are maybe
3-4-5
And you count
1,2,3,4,5 10-12-19
Cause...
That's the way sometime
They come, when
You are maybe
3-4-5
And that's the way you count
Till another day
When,
The numbers come another
Way
Like 1-2-3-4-5-6-7-8-9-10
And...
You´re older then.

In The Park

A day in the park
And sunshiny too
Where families
Are roaming
With children there too
Is a most wonderful
Place
To just be there
And see
Just wonderful
Beautiful happiness there be
From...
A day in the park
With and where
Families together
And-just
Sunshiny be.

Tonight

Its cold tonight
The clouds are low
Some clouds are dark
Some clouds are
Orange.
The sky is kind of
Hazy bluish blue
Its cold tonight
I think
Don´t you?

The Way

Sometime the numbers
You count
Seem to come
When you are maybe
3-4-5
And you count
1,2,3,4,5 10-12-19
Cause...
That's the way sometime
They come, when
You are maybe
3-4-5
And that's the way you count
Till another day
When,
The numbers come another
Way– like 1-2-3-4 all the way,
To one hundred.
And...
You´re older then.

Picture

A picture you gave me (of you)
When first we met
I have with me yet
And will have it with me
All my days.
It was with me-all the
58 years of our marriage
Was with me enlarged
For all to see
When you were called
By the creator.
Is with me now-on the wall
It stays-I see it
When I exercise each morning
Of every day.
The picture (of you) you gave me
When first-we met.

Leave

When you must leave
I will love you too
With a love
That's deep
Always
And true.
In my heart...
Always
True.

Cocoa

The boys, they are
Making cocoa
From
Water,sand,
And mud today
It will maybe
Surely be
Quite different,
When they finish
With it...
Their way.

When

When the wife was there
She could be in the living room
And I in the bedroom
Outside or somewhere
But I knew she was there
She the same I´m sure
We knew the other was-there near
But now she´s gone forever
Now there's a lonesome.
The place is an empty shell
Sometimes late at night
Because I doze on the sofa
Or something-time passes
Till almost day-someway
Since she left most everyday
And at times I find my self
Just hollering or screaming
At myself.
And I wonder why this happens
As time goes by.
Perhaps it happens to others
That their past has then happened to come
take them to places.
This I wonder, I ponder, I wonder
I wonder this I do
As hours pass by.
This I feel in my make up is
Passing by but its a stage of
Grieving I feel that must pass-thru
I believe the mourning the feeling
Of my wife of 58 years will never
Fully pass and I never want it
To fully pass-our love for each other
was deep-it grew with our
Family-our years.
And this I feel is natural to
Feel this way.
And I do-its healthy to
Grieve mourn
My wife I´m sure wants me too
If she were here I would want
Her to grieve. I think all are different
But I´m sure all who love truly
Are lonesome. When one, leaves one.

The Ball

You...
Bounce the ball
Real high to me,
See how high
It will go and
When it comes
Down to me
I´ll try to catch it
If I can
If I can´t thats ok
When I get it
I´ll bounce it back
To you
I´ll bounce it real
High too
Let´s do that
Ok?

Noisy

There´s a noisy
Airplane in the sky
Hiding in the clouds
As it flies by
I wonder if
That noisy airplane
Hiding in the clouds
Flying by.
Knows I hear it
But don´t see it
Hiding in the clouds
In the sky.

A Happy Game

One day...there was
The wind-the clouds
And a bird
In the sky
And the wind
Blew the bird
Across the sky
Right under
The clouds that
Were in the sky.
And the wind
And the bird
And the clouds
Played a happy game,
In the sky
That day.

Birdhouse

Hang a bird house
In a tree
Hope a bird-will come
And see,
And live
In the bird house
You hanged
In the tree
That would-be so nice
To see
A bird-living
In the bird house
You hanged
In a tree.

To See

Blossoms, blossoms
On our apple tree
May soon-make apples
Grow on, our apple tree
And it would be
Nice
To see-apples grow
On our apple tree
Where now
Blossoms only
There we see.

A Nice Day

Today is a
A little bit hazy
But not too much
A little bit cloudy
With a sun seeking
touch
A little bit cool
When the wind blows
Thru.
But today is a nice day.
I like it
Too.

A Walk Today

Went for a walk
Today
With children of ages
About 3 or 4 some 5
We went for a walk
Their way
Picked up flowers,
Some old-some new
A few leaves
And sticks
That they threw
Collected too.
Played games-threw bounce balls
Took over a,
Tennis court
Occupied it too,
Our way.
We had much fun
On our walk today
With children...
Of ages,
3-4 some 5,
When we went
For a walk...
Their way.

Climbed

I climbed
Up a ladder
Down the ladder
Across another
Ladder
Up another ladder
Down the ladder
I got off
And ran,
Do it if you can
I dare you?

Are Nice

Onions,
Onions are nice
They usually come
In colors of
White-green
or kind of
Blue
You can use them
In salads
Soups
Many ways
Cook with en too
And if you´re not
A good cook
Like me
They make you
Cry a little
When you cut them,
Too
Least me
They do.
But onions
Are nice
And come
Usually
In colors
Of
White-green
Or kind of,
Blue.

Good Friends

Night time
Its a nice time too
Cause-twilight's finished
Evening too
Stars come out
The moon peeps thru
Stars and moon
Up there
Doin what they
Have to do.
They stay till dawn
And till day
Comes thru
Till night time
Again.
So, night times
A really nice time
Cause-its... a,
Real good friend,
With daytime
Too.

Lets Go

I see a little white house
With a green-and white
Door
I wonder what's inside
Lets go see
Maybe there's-an old
Witch,
Maybe-Cinderella's
There
Let's open-the little
Green and white
Door
Lets look in
And see
Ok.
Oh, nobody's here at least
Not today.

Will Do

Wet-wet
And
Wetter too
Water
Can do that
To you
Rain-buckets
Pans-cups
Any amount
Of water
Can make you
Wet-wet
And
Wetter too
If you like it
If you don´t
Water can
And
Water will
Make you
Wet wet
And
Wetter too
More and more
Of water
Will do, that
To you.

8 Bicycles

We have 8 bicycles
Altogether
I see 4 bicycles
Over there
I see 1 bicycle
There
That is 5 bicycles
Right,
There is 2 more
Bicycles over there
That is 7 bicycles
One is missing,
Oh now I see it,
That little boy is
Riding it
Now we have 8 bicycles
Altogether,
In this poem
With you...
And me.

Of Blue

A drifting cloud
In a sky of blue
Just moving by
So you can see it
Too.
Is restful, and nice
If you can
Spare a few
Moments of
Your-self busied
Day
And watch a
Part of the world
Pass thru
For you-its...
Way.
In
A drifting cloud
And,
The sky-of blue.

Gardens

Plant the seed
Water the seed
Watch the garden grow
Garden´s are a
Lot of fun
Fun and work
Make food...
For everyone.
Just plant the seed –water the seed,
Watch the garden grow.

Round and Round

The wind-the Wind
Turned rapidly- one day
Round and round
Till it reached
The ground, far below
Where it picked up a house
And a car below
And it tore up the car
Moved the house
In pieces and pieces
To far, very far away
As quick as a wink
One day.
And...
A baby was sleeping
In a bed
Where it lay
Not awakened from
Its sleep
On that windy day the wind
Turned, round and round
Till it reached, the ground
That day-that windy day.

Mr. Moon

Old Mr. moon
Tho mysterious
And far away
Causes much
Of what we do
And have to say
The way we plant
The tides
Even weather
Crops too
Old Mr. moon
Mysterious and...far away.
Far, far away.

A Week

Today is Saturday
And,
Seven days, passed by-
Gosh...
A week-just finished, when-
Today,
Went on its
Merry way.

Notes

The notes of a song
Of a story-too
Goes on and on
To the ears
Of, the
Attentive
And on, and on
To other´s
Of the same
Heard various
Ways
For days
And days
And years
And days
Yes-oh yes
The notes of a song
Of story.too
Goes on and on
Thru various
Ways,
And on.

Home

The house-the house
With no electric
Kerosene lamp lights
Hand pump for water
Small-in the country
A, 2 room house
Where I was born
I will always
Remember
That little house
Way-way
In the quiet
Country
It was a
Happy happy
Child hood home...
There.
Out in the quiet,
Of the near- tho
Faraway.

The Moon

If you-could
Sleep sleep
Till afternoon
And go
To the moon
Where there´s
Lots of room
And play
Basket ball
Foot ball
Base ball
Soccer
All day-any day
All night, too be nice-
Maybe...
If you sleep
Till noon
And find a way
You could
Get to the moon
And take
Basketballs-footballs
Baseballs and
Soccer balls
With you
When you go there
Too.

Loves There

Hop scotch-is a game
That children play
As they grow, as they grow
Their childhood way
And
They mingle with others
Grow with others
Mix with others
In their way-study with others
Various studies
As they grow
Traveling on-and thru
Life's road
And, all the way
Meeting love-greeting love
Children, others
Thru
Faith-families
Too
Even, as comes
Understanding- misunderstanding
Light, dark
Lightning-thunder
Rainbows
Crying, flowers
Also-leaving
Loves there-all the way thru
Quite...
Like hop scotch is
A game
Children play-adults too
Their way, their choice
In life
As they grow-as we grow
With the creators love
Always, there sustaining
As we grow.

Of Flowers

As above the sunrise, of
Far away-there's always
Memories to remember of-
Each yesterday
Like fields of flowers
Woven thru dreams
Rainbows, butterflies
All it seems,
Storms are there
Fair weather too.
But above the sunrise
As the sun shines thru
There's blue of sky
From far away.
With love that flows
Spiritually bright
Mid holidays near
With special love, thru-
Forever
And...
Memories usually have room-for the lovely too.
With light…
As above the sunrise
All,
Just for you.

Always There

The cold of winters left
The flowers have returned
The birds came too
And blossoms came thru
Tho winter was long
Holding on and on
Continuously
Till light thru love
Released all-in a silent way.
The blossoming of
an eternal day.
And now...
The winter
The flowers, birds
The blossoms
And love
Build memories-blended with forever
As beautiful
Rainbows after a storm
Of always near.
Spiritual-beautiful
Lovely.
Now that
The cold of winters left.

Thru Love

There is connection
I believe-as a star
That guides
When we ask
Whether near
Or from far
Tho not to see, but
To believe
Is so free
There is a connection
I believe
That guides when asked
Thru love-for all,
Creations love...from a far.

Comprehend

Its hard for we to comprehend
The rays of rising sun
Or things its rays
Just mean to us
Each one by chosen one
Its hard for we to comprehend
Each noon time, twilight evening too.
Or seconds, minutes, hours
Days or years, as we
That thru them stray.
But as the sun that gives us light
Also stars that twinkle-oh so bright
The moon with shimmering
Silvery light.
The creations creator with
Eternal guiding light
Guides us spiritually
In all we ask, seek and do
And comprehends, rewards
As warm rays of rising sun
With guiding love to us
Faithfully all the way everyday.
Tho, its hard for we to comprehend
We pray for you
And your family, and-
Prayers power, has...no end.

Of Love

Mountains are difficult
Hard to climb
But at the top, there´s brilliant
Bright sunshine
Clouds on the way-hard to see thru
Help mountains appear-anywhere too.
But if theres a will
To climb to the top
To see thru the fog
To see thru the dark
To dream of the day
To dream of a way.
Where sunshine of day
Will light a path way
To head on ward and thru
And change the way.
That love can flow.
Then, mountains can be path´s of healing eternal
love...
To heaven high.

Thru the Years

As mountains
Rise to the heavens
And oceans
Cover miles untold.
As sun lights
The sky by day.
And moon
Among stars...
The heavens
By night.
Building trust
Love
And hope.
As centuries
Unfold.
May your faith
Build spiritual
Love
Hope
And trust.
Thru the years...
As the years
With beauty
Unfold.

Mistake

To have made
A mistake
And all is
Still ok,
Is to have
Learned something...
The mistake,
Has made-
For better,
Days.

The Wind

Oh kite
As you fly
In the Wind
On your string.
The tug that
You give
On the string,
Is a joy-too –to the one
And a school
To the one
That made you.
Oh kite
As you fly
And you tug
On your string
In the wind.

Chimes

Even at noon
When sunshine shadows fall soft
And off toward twilight time
Down hall ways-cross meadows
Cross fields cross the far away
And near
Chimes sound thru invisible air
Ringing-chiming from all around
The hours are yours
The hours are mine
They chime so free-so close
The sounds
Touch-see-hear-feel
The chiming-ringing-bringing
Each dawn-noon-twilight evening
Eternal...to surround.
Silent chimes the chimes, chimes of love.
And are musically lovely –also
Ever present as
Drifting clouds in skies of blue
Thru faith above.

The Rain

Hide me from
The rain
Where oh where?
Hide me from
The rain
The rain´s looking
For me
The rains looking
For me
Hide me from
The rain
Where oh where
The rains every where
Hide me-hide me
Just...
Hide me from the rain
The rain-the rain
Its looking, its looking
Its looking
Its looking for me
I know-its-its looking for me
Ok, ok, ok-we´ll just,
Wait till
The rainbow comes
And we´ll hide you
Right out in the sun
Because...
The sun never comes
At the
Time of the rain
And the
Rain never comes
At the
Time of the sun
Their times-to stay
Are never-the same
So we will hide you
Right out in the sun

continued

Ok, ok, ok
I´ll hide from the rain
In the sun
All day
Then go home
At the end of the day
Thank you, thank you
And have a nice day
All day
Then go home
At the end of the day
Thank you, thank you
And have a nice day
All day
Your way
Out in the sun
And have...
Fun.

Years Past

My friend collects
Old toy trucks
And toys
I guess they tell him
His way
Of gone by-years past
Days.
A mystery the toys
Of now-and all,
Will get for free
In years
Is...
Years past days.
But
My friend collects then
And en joys...
Trucks, toys
Of by gone,
Years past
Days.

Flowers

Plant the flowers
Water the flowers
Pick the flowers
Sometime
Too. (flowers are pretty)
I like flowers
Don´t you,
Too?

The Mountain

Alone...
At the mountain top
When a child
Is born-is when
Reality starts
a new life
Is here
As a brand new year
Is for me
Its for me to rear
To start on the way to
to teach a child.
Include
As I travel
Life's way
The same as before
Only now
There is more
For another watches
And learns everyday
As we together-travel
Life's
Lengthy road, rocky
And smooth highway
The schools of training
Sacrifice-thru diligent
Honest work
Days, weeks, months
Years...
That will pass
Before
The child, to adult
Will be-and pass to
Be a, good community
Productive-citizen
I've-my family
And all-can be
Proud of
And I, we
Years later
Can be once again
Alone...
At the mountain top.

Comprehend

Its hard for we to comprehend
The rays of rising sun
Or things its rays
Just mean to us
Each one by chosen one
Its hard for we to comprehend
Each noon time, twilight evening too.
Or seconds, minutes, hours
Days or years, as we
That thru them stray.
But as the sun that gives us light
Also stars that twinkle-oh so bright
The moon with shimmering
Silvery light.
The creations creator with
Eternal guiding light
Guides us spiritually
In all we ask, seek and do
And comprehends, rewards
As warm rays of rising sun
With guiding love to us
Faithfully all the way everyday.
Tho, its hard for we to comprehend
We pray for you
And your family, prayers
Reach, thru silently.

Gone

The past is gone
Its gone to stay
The future-comes new
And stays
One day-everyday
But...
May last, and last, outlast-
The past- its way.

Of Love

Mountains are difficult
Hard to climb
But at the top, there´s brilliant
Bright sunshine
Clouds on the way-hard to see thru
Help mountains appear-anywhere too.
But if there's a will
To climb to the top
To see thru the fog
To see thru the dark
To dream of the day
To dream of a way.
Where sunshine of day
Will light a path way
To head on ward and thru
And change the way.
That love can flow.
Then, mountains can be path´s of healing eternal
love...
To heaven high.

On Days

Sometimes
At times-on days
One gets
So very tired
Of doing things
The way-they´re
Not supposed
To be done,
At times
On those days.
And after
Much thinking
One says.
Hah...
Now I know why,
Its not suppose
To be done
That way.

Slow

Snails go slow
So very slow.
And take their house
And leave a shiny path,
Everywhere-
They go.

Sunshine

The sunshine
Went
With the clouds
To stay.
But might come back-
Later on,
Today.

Can See

I wanted to write this
Before - why I didn´t
I really don´t know why.
Guess maybe it was
Because the mountain
Was so high.
As it was before.
I can see the top
And over,
Where there´s sunshine
A tree, and room, also bright
Warm too.
Silently saying, come - look,
Stay for a while and-
Leave when you want to
Thank you for really
Helping me thru.
When the mountain
Was very high
And the lonesome
Was too.
Now that I finally
Wrote this,
I feel better-
I really do.

Gone

You can call it
What you may
But its really
Good to know and feel
That your loved one's are
Even tho – they´re gone
Are there with you
When you call or need
Them - in your very-
Special way - anytime
Any day - and you
Can silently count on
Them - to help things
Flow along that´s good
For you - with you
Tho they´re gone
In silence
Their non existent way,
Only you understand-
But it helps.

The Clouds

Where did the clouds go
They were here
Just a few minutes ago
Now I see blue sky everywhere
Look...
Can´t you see, blue sky too
Yes,
I can see blue sky.
Oh the clouds-
They´ll come back
They always do
But today,
I see blue sky
And sunshine too-
Lets have a nice day
Today.
And when the clouds
Come back,
We´ll have a nice day
That day-
Too.

The Sunshine

Hey...
Here comes the sunshine
There goes the clouds
And I can see blue sky
Too.
Maybe we can still...
Have the picnic
Go to the park
Have a really nice day
I think - don´t you -
Cause...
Here comes the sunshine
There goes the clouds
And...
I can see blue sky
Too.

Thank You

Just thank you
Is so nice to say
And should come
From some where
Everyday.
Its so nice to hear
And then to be
The some one
You can say – "yes"
"Oh-yes"...
That thank you
Came from-
Me.

For You

Isn´t it strange
What a song - can do for you
Just remember
And sing soft, so soft
Any old song
You remember-
Familiar to you.
And it will take you back
In your mind
To places
And times-to remember
Where you used to be,
For free.
Isn´t it strange...
What a song, can do - with your mind,
For you.

A Crow

Over there is a crow
Sitting on a pole
So high.
There is only
Clouds and a little rain
Between-
The crow
And...the sky

Waves

The ocean waves
So quiet can be
And with moonlight too
Speak romantically
But with earthquake
Mixed...
And with anger too
Can...
Create tsunami,
Great
With waves of water
Large...
Destroying creations
Wondrous life and land-
Then...
Become again,
The ocean waves
Quiet, as quiet be,
And with moonlight too
Speak romantically...
The ocean, the ocean
The ocean
With waves-
Of mysterious,
The ocean.

Except

I guess
There's other folks, like me
Today with nothing to do
Except sit
In a restaurant
And watch the cars
I see go by.
And think...
Now
There must be
Something better
Today...
That folks like me-
Could do.

Take

Take your medicine
So you can be
That of what
You want
To see.
Take your medicine
And you are
To others - who they see
And...
As they see
You are,
Medicine is
And
Medicine does
And fixes
Perhaps...
The you - for you
You think-
You was.

Many Things

Mountains - mountains
Most times
We see them - from
Far far away
Or some time
We see them close by
Where they stay.
Tho they are
Far far away
Or right close too.
And its seldom
We touch them.
Mountains, mountains
Are in-
Many things,
That we do.

About

Its ok to cry
When you have to.
To let
Something, someone
Or
Whatever
Out.
Or try- to cry
To shout,
To be - or let you be,
The you
That you´re
Suppose to be
About.

I See

In the sky,
Of blue
Tonight.
I see-
A quarter moon
And stars of bright
Shining, with
-Just heavenly
Light.

A Connection

Some how
There's a connection
Between those who´ve left
And those that's here
That exists some how.
At times I can feel it.
They converse
Some how at times
I can hear their
Guiding voice,
I can feel it
Especially if their
Picture is near - where I can see.
Some say its imagination
I don´t really know
But...
Some how
there's a connection
And for me its good
Very good
Fills the lonesome
With a love
Some how.

Wind

The trees are
Moving, moving
The wind is going thru,
I cannot see the wind.
Can you, can you,
Can you?

My Knee

One night after dark - I placed my cap
Upon my head, and sat-
With pad, down - to write words,
Them, to be read
Then - placed my cap
Upon my knee
Under the pad I used
To write upon with paper
There words to see.
I felt the cap slip
From knee to floor
But upon the floor, not anywhere
I could not find - my cap,
My cap upon the floor.
Found it tho - in a closet near
Yes closet near with closed...
With closed of door.
And i placed it my cap
Upon my knee, and felt it slip
From knee to floor.
Then found it not upon the floor
But in a closet with closed door.
How could this be - when only
One night after dark, I placed my cap
Upon my knee.
This of the strange, how could this be
But this - yes this
It happened to me
When I placed my cap
Upon my knee.

Autumn

A falling leaf
Just struck me.
It came from a tree
Over there.
Leaves are falling
It seems-
Everywhere.
The cool of,
Season´s
Autumn...
Is in the air.

Passing Thru

Sunday afternoon
And a cloudy day too
Not many cars
On the street with people,
Passing thru
Guess they´re all
In houses - or somewhere,
Tucked away
Cause...
This, Sunday afternoon
And being
A cloudy day too
Not many cars
On the street - with people
Passing thru.

158

Quiet

Sssh-sssh-sssh
Be quiet as can be
Everybody's sleeping
Or can´t you see
I´m trying to sleep
So don't´ wake me
Sssh-sssh-sssh
Please-
Be quiet as can be.

The World

Help someone
In a way
So others will
Never know,
Or understand
That day
You helped-someone in the
The world to be,
A better -boy, girl-
woman or man-in the world.

All Day

Sunshine's out
Gonna stay all day
Clouds gone
Sun´s here today
Blue sky soon
A really nice day
Cause...
Sunshine's out-
Gonna stay all day.

To Do

To run
To hop
To skip
To jump
Is good
For you
To do.
Do you
Like
To run, to hop, to skip, to jump----?
Its good
For you
To do.

Rainy

Today's
A rainy cloudy day
No sunshine
In the sky today
Just a rainy
Cloudy sky
To show us all
Where the sunshine
Was.

Over There

"Hey", lets go see
What they're doin
Over there
Looks like they're
Havin a lot of fun
Over there.
Hear all the music
And a singin
And a dancin,
Children playin too-
Sounds like they're
Havin-a real good
Time over there
Why – they're...
Right over yonder
On that hill over there.
Lets go see,
What they're doin
Over there.

Kind Of

Music of old
Maybe 30-40
Years or more
Heard today
Kind of makes
And sets
The mood
Of...
Times past
And of today
For it fits
Both much
Of times past
A little
Small bits-of today
Kind of
Then silently
Fades away
Music of old
Maybe 30-40
Years or more
Heard today.

Turkey Buzzards

I see
Turkey buzzards
Turkey buzzards
In a big tree
Flying in
Flying out
Just to see
What they can see.

On Days

Sometimes...
At times-on days
One gets
So very tired
Of
Doing things
The way-they're
Not supposed
To be done
At times
On those days
And after
Much thinking
One says
Hah...
Now
I know why.

Gone

The past is gone
Its gone to stay
The future comes new
And stays.
One day, everyday
May last - and last
As new
Tho past.

Are

Religions, religions,
So many they are
Folks preach
And
They teach, and do
And if we don't
Watch out
There goes another war
Where we must do
What we can
Till its thru
Trying
To understand
The many teachings,
Religions –do for,
They are
Near and far

The Clouds

Where did the clouds go
They were here
Just a few minutes ago
Now I see blue sky everywhere
Look...
Can it you see, blue sky too
Yes,
I can see blue sky.
Oh the clouds-
They'll come back
They always do
But today,
I see blue sky
And sun shine too-
Lets have a nice day
Today.
And when the clouds
Come back,
We'll have a nice day that day-
Too.

Life's Puzzle

There´s part of life's puzzle
That you fill
No body else can do
Tho you´re gone
You always will be there
For that part remains,
There still.
Its part of life
That was - that is-
That always forever will be
A part and of the you
A part and of the me
That's a part of life's puzzle
That was meant
Thru deep love...
To forever –and ever
be.

.

A Pretty Bird

Now seagulls they´re a pretty bird
They have feet like ducks
To stop in trees.
They´re out of luck
But they can swim
And dive-
Catch fish too
Fly real high-up in the sky
And soar so beautiful
When they fly high
They look like-small airplanes
Just floating-in the sky.
Hardly moving their wings
When they fly.
Now seagulls are-
A strange a mysterious
And a pretty bird too
Also water´s
Not too far
When you see them
Pass thru.

Your World

In your world-what do you see
And who stays-in the world
Where you stay
Does a voice speak to you
In your world
If it does-what to you
Does it say
Does it whisper—does it talk
Does it to you, silent
But happiness-bring
In your world does rippling-
Waters soft beneath twilight-
Faint of rain by glow
Give love-to you-alone
The love-love brings
The world we see
That world must be
Our world...
The world that brings
Us thru-
In all we do
No matter who.

Birds

Not even one bird
In the tree today
Not even one bird
Near the tree today
Just why did the birds
All go away
From the tree
That I see
Right today over there near me
Today.
Where are the birds
Just where are the birds
Where are the birds
Today
Not even one bird
In the tree
Today.

Standing

The moon was standing
In the bright sun light
Right left to the center
Of the sky.
I seen it standing
As bright as could be
I see it with my own
Naked eye.
The sky was blue
A really deep blue
As clouds were few
In the sky.
While the moon
Was standing
In the bright sun light
Right left to the center
Of the sky.
I wonder why.

Clouds to Cover

The clouds are coming
The clouds are coming
I know they are coming
I see the clouds coming
Now...
There's blue in the sky to see.
But the clouds are going
Where ever they please.
They're starting way over
There over the top
Of the far away trees.
And soon they'll cover
The blue in the sky
And they will be soon-soon
All over the sky.
The clouds are coming
The clouds are coming
I know they are coming
To cover...
To cover the sky.

Barking

Wolves bark
At the moon
When they want to-
And the moon I think,
Answers them-in its way too.
And people do.
When they're lone some
Holler like wolves
At the moon
Or any thing-or nothing
When they're there lone some
And no ones there
To hear them
And its quiet
Cause.
Believe it or not
People are animals
And...
Wolves may have
Come across
Something good to do
To relieve themselves
When, they're barking,
About something
Just or barking-
At the moon
When they want to.

My Sunshine

Tho you are gone
From here-far away
You light up my life
Like day light-each day
You are my sunshine
Oh yes
Where you are
From for away
You are my sunshine
Tho gone away
You are my sunshine
You are
Every day.

Here

Not here
You´re gone away
I can hear the words
You say
And they guide
Like a far off star
Tho you´re gone
Are here-The words
From far,
And...
Thanks.

A Nest

I watched a bird
Making a nest
Working so hard
Making a nest
Taking a piece of grass
It could find
A leaf a straw
Of almost any kind.
And almost anything
Too went there,
When it was finished
I wonder if-
And if its needed.
There will be-
A door-tho
I´m sure the bird
Thought of that,
Before.

Big Sky

One cloud only
In a big sky of blue
Drifting this way
That way too
Where will it go
And what will it do
And how will it know
When it gets-where
Its going to.
Should a soft breeze
Help it-on its way
Or best let it drift
Go where it may
One cloud only
One cloud only
One cloud only
In a big sky of blue.

Maybe

There is another world
At times-I think
That is, that´s maybe-
Quite, like this
Where minds of kind
Or such-of much
May think-the same
As we-at times
And contacts
Here-with us
To warn and keep us
Informed
Of that-of good-or bad
With love
There is another world
At times-I think
That is-that´s maybe-
Quite, like this.

Graceful

Seagull´s...
Wings of white,
Over water
Over land
Are graceful-
In flight

Ran

The little boy ran
Thru the building
Out the door
Across the bridge
And on to the playground
He wasn´t the
First there
He wasn´t the
Last there
But he was there
I seen him there
The little boy
Who ran.

Autumn Wind

The windy, windy
Autumn wind
Is blowing leaves
On trees
And the leaves are falling
Soft soft down
Down-down
And to the ground
As the November
Windy autumn
Wind
Blow and blows
Today.

Vulture

There's a vulture
Sitting on a pole
And I think
He´s looking right at me
I don´t know why
He´s sitting there
I guess to stare.

Flew

The butterfly
Flew by
And flew into
The blue
Of the sky
And I never more
Seen...
The butterfly.

A Treasure

There's a treasure
Buried near here
My friend told me
I´m sure its true
He said the pirates
Buried it when
They were passing thru.
And forgot the place
They buried it
They had so much to do
My friend.
He made a treasure map
I seen him make, the map
So when we find, the treasure
We´ll just take-
The pirate ship,
With us-too.

With Voice

A scream
A call
A voice, from-
Inside
May sometime
Come from
Deep within
To let the
Feelings from
Within-come out
And-let
Deep feelings out
Be not alarmed
It makes away
To be for with-
Voice, much better days
We see
As days and days
There be.

On

The seconds-they make
The minutes
The minutes-the hours
And hours-noons
Afternoons-twilight
Evenings-nights
Dawns-days
And days-they make
Weeks, months, years
Years-they make...
The ageless
Ages
While seconds move countless
Tho
Eternally
On.
And...
Into forever

Remarkable

Brains, brains, brains
Brains, brains, brains
Brains are funny things
And they work in funny ways
And they do remarkable
Amazing, sometime dangerous things
Those brains, brains, brains
Its amazing how we train
Those brains, brains, brains
And remarkable too
The things we do
When we train
The...
Brain, brain, brain
And then...
The ways we our find
These brains, brains, brains.
They do remarkable things.

Right

That what is right
Is not only what
Is in sight.
What is right
Must be
The should
What would
And will be,
Eventually.
If all is judged
As should be.
The right
For...right
Is right
And always
Must be,
Eternally.

The Sun

A little boy-said to me
The sun is coming out
The sun is coming out
Who-eee, who-eee, who-eee
The sun is coming out
No more inside for me, I see
The sun is coming out
The sun is coming out
Who-eee, who-eee, who-eee,
The sun is coming out
And he was very happy, too
That day
As he
Passed by, going
Thru. Happiness...
Has it's ways.

Told

I was a little
Bad today the little boy said,
Not a whole
Bunch tho.
Now I can't play
On the playground
Now
The teacher told
Me so.

Get Thru

Say...I´ve got
No where to go, so
I don´t go any where
I´ve got no one-
To talk to-so
I talk to my self
Till I´m thru
I stay up late-till
Mornings here
Maybe its cause
With no where to go
No one to talk to
You never-ever really get thru doing
Just doing that too.

Why Didn't

Why didn´t
I think of that before
It was so easy too
Now I´ve got
The rest of the day
To do-the things
That I must do
And help better
The days, go thru
Why didn´t
I think of that before
My my
Why didn´t I.

Go

Obey and go
Even tho
You do not know
The why or the where
You are told to do
You will be told
When the time is right
You will understand
When the time is right
Believe and go
Okay and go
Even tho-
You now
Do not know
The reasons are many
As stars in the sky
Beautifully, beautiful
Heavens, high.

Highway

Walking life's highway
Early each morning
As the sun rises
In the sky
That bright ball of
Sun light...
Lights both smooth
And rough places
On life's high way
As one walks
Each morning
And thru the day-
On life's
Eternal...
High way.

A Sparrow

Small as a sparrow
The bird
It be
It has a place
In creation,
As we
And is missed
Some where...
If the sparrow-
We do not see.

Sunshine

Oh say-
The sunshine-went away
With the clouds
To stay, for a-
Little while,
Today.
And it might come back
Later on,
Later on-today.

Slow

Snails more slow
Very, very slow
And take their house
And leave
A shiny, shiny
Path
Everywhere
They go.

Buttons

Buttons buttons
Clothes like buttons
Round buttons
Square buttons
Small buttons
Large buttons too.
Buttons, buttons
Clothes like buttons
Do you too?

Leave

When you must leave
I will love you too
With a love
That's deep
With in my heart
And always
True.

Rat Cat Wind

The little blue cat
Sat on a hat
In the wind
And a rat ran by
Chasing a fly
That flew very fast
Passing by
A cloud covering
The blue of sky
While a quarter moon
Stood silent
Far far off
In the light of a
Moon-light noon
Day time sky moved.
And the little blue cat
Still sat on a hat
In the Wind
While the rat
Ran fast, fast faster
Chasing a small
Noisy buzzing
Fly, my, my, why.

You

If...
I choose to leave
And you´re there
I
Will wait,
Till you return,
If..
I must leave
The choice was mine,
Either way.
It, was my
Desire.
Don´t worry-
You were on
My mind.
You were there
In love...
I chose to leave
And you
Were there.
I left, because I had to,
But I Love You.

You See

Some things in life
Only you see
Others are there
But they only be.
For-
Some things in life
Only you see
Its meant to be
That way
And that way...
It be.

Show

Religions, religions
They´re different-you know
They cause you to do
They cause you to act
As so,
This is good-that is bad
That is ok-this is not
Depends where you are
And how you do
What´s been done by you
Whether good or bad
Religions, religions
They´re different you know
And cause the world
To put on its really
Great lovely a show.

Everyone

When we see
Someone
Where before-
There was two
And now there is
Always-
Only one-
You never can know
How really
Lone some
Is
Till you cxpcrience
The daily feeling
Of one and
Daily-
Only one.
Make merry
In someway
Everyday
For all, so someone… you know,
And, one lonesome
May have that experience
Sometime

Today

Sing a song
Any old song
Any song
That you really want to
Hum a song
Whistle a song
Make some music
Your way
It will make you
Feel happy
It will make you
Feel good
It helps slip slide time-
In a very special way.
Sing a song
Any old song-any old song
Today.

Over There

The clouds are coming
Over the building top
Over the building top
Way over there
I wonder why
Why are the clouds
Coming this was
This way today
From way over there.
Do you think they´re
Coming to say hello
Or cover the sun
All day-and go.
And maybe snow.
But-look-look
The clouds are coming
Over the building top
Way over there.
I wonder why.

The Wind

If...
You could-
See the wind
And
The Wind
Could see you
Do you think
The wind would be-
An animal
Like you and me too?
Just...
What might it be
If the wind,
We could
See.

Near There

There's a treasure
Buried near here
My friend told me
I´m sure its true.
He said the pirates
Buried it-
And left their ship
When they were
Passing thru.
And that they also
Forgot the place
They buried the treasure
They had so much to do.
My friend...
He made a treasure map
I seen him do it too
And said we could
Go find the treasure
When we do-
you can just bet
We´ll take the pirates
Ship with us too.

Windy

The flowers are
Moving
The trees are
Moving
The clouds are
Moving too.
Its windy today-
And the wind,
Is passing
Thru.

Bed

Always remember
When you get up
To make your bed
In the morning
It puts some order
In your day
to make your bed
in...
the morning-the morning
when you get up
each day.

My Knee

One night after dark
I placed my cap
Open my head-and sat down
With pad to write words
Then to be read
Then placed my cap
Upon my knee
Under the pad- I used
To write upon with paper
There words to see.
I felt the cap
Slip from knee to floor
And the floor, the floor, upon the floor
Not anywhere
I could not find, my cap
My cap upon the floor.
But found it in a closet
Near-with closed, yes closed
Of door.
Tho I placed it there-my cap
Upon my knee, and felt it
Slip from knee to floor
And found it not-upon the floor
But in a closet with closed door
How could this be, how could this be
This of the strange
How could this be when only
One night while writing after dark
I placed my cap upon my knee
Tis strange-tis strange
And maybe the strange
Where-are they be...
They smile too-with almost glee.

Night Sky

High in the sky
With its light
Going by
An airplane flies-
Seen quite like a star
In the night
Time sky.

November

Its November today
And I watched
As the wind gently
Blew its way
While leaves of a tree
Drifted down
And a little boy-and
A little girl
Of maybe three and a half
Four or fire
Happened by-and watched as I-
The action
Of Novembers wind
Causing the leaves to fall
Gently down-to the ground
I asked of the two
Did you see the wind?
The little boy said yes
The wind is small
The little girl said
The wind is blue
I told them both
Thank you
They went on their way
I watched,
As the wind blew
And...
Its November today.

Moves

As we go...
No matter
How fast,
No matter
How slow,
Our shadow-
Moves with us
Wherever...
We-go...

173

Today

Yesterday
The wind blew
Leaves on trees
Yesterday
The wind blew
A kite
Up high
Yesterday
The wind blew
Birds
In the sky
Yesterday
The wind blew
A sail boat by.
Today-
Where is the wind?
Can you see the wind?
Where
Oh where
Is the wind.
Today?

Silence

The beauty of silence
Where we can not hear
The noise or commotion
That is always near
Can be chaotic...it can be
As beauty of
Clouds adrift-
In a heaven of blue
The beholder of
Silence,
This alone can feel
Or see
With this-only this
The beauty, of silence
Can be.

Fall

Our friend
The ground
Will catch you
No matter
From how high-or way
You fall
The ground will always
Catch you
Just feel free
To-
Fall
Fall
Fall.

Hides

The wind is passing thru
Look, look
See what it can do
It moves the leaves
On trees
It bends the grass
Down low.
And makes a whirl wind
Too
For all to see
And all this free
Yet hides and hides
Right by your side
And the wind-
No one,
Can ever-ever,
See.
The wind, the wind is passing thru

Greedy-Greedy

Greed-greed-greed
Maybe if we´re honest
Maybe just a wee bit
Just little bitty bit
Honest.
We´re all just a
Little bit greedy
Where we greed
Can real, real, quiet hide
Like in our secret quiet
Or-with,
Or best, best, friends
Reside
Perhaps, it could be found
Psst-psst-hey, what's your
Pet greed?
Huh-oh that
Didn´t know
It was still a round
That's a funny one
(Ha-ha)

We See

If you could see
Everything
I can see
And,
I could see
Every thing
You can see
We could see everything
Two times
We see.
That would be nice
Or would it, be-
Of everything
We see
What do you think?
Would it be?

Seagull

A white seagull
In a deep blue sky
Is real pretty
To see-
Flying by.

To Enjoy

I see clouds-in the sky
I see white clouds
In the sky
I see one, no-two
White seagulls, flying
In front of
The white clouds
In the sky
I see a blue sky-behind
The white
Clouds in the sky
I see sunshine too
I see a lovely day
Passing thru
And...
I see white clouds
I see white clouds
And sea gulls
In a blue blue sky.
All there
For every one
And me
To enjoy-
On high.

Why

Whiskey stores
Guns and drugs
Where do you find em
More and more
Most in places-
Poor folks stay
Seems they're
Put there
There to stay.
Most folks wish-they'd
Go away
Cause they make families troubles
Come and stay
Whiskey stores, and guns
And drugs
Find em there where
Poor folks stay
Why oh why
Does it seem-happens that way
Wish I knew.
All's I got to say.

Workin

Yuh first start working
When you're old enough
Then yuh can't stop working
When yer old enough
Cause if yuh do
Yer body don't really really
Want yuh to
So yuh keep on workin
Workin, workin
Till you've had enough
Like-
Yuh first started workin
When yer old enough.

Thru Too

There's a place-in the road
That you travel too
Where one that
Helped you thru
Where you're gotten too
Leaves you
Then you-realize
I am at that place
In the road
We have traveled there
I must go on
To the place
We were going
Thru, too.

Windy

Its windy its windy
Its windy today
And the birds are flying
They're flying today.
The wind blows-the birds
This way-that way too
For the wind is strong
Blows the birds along
Everywhere-where it goes,
In the air.
Cause
Its windy its windy
Its windy today.

Passing Thru

I think maybe
The leaves are tired
They are drifting down
To rest for winter
On the ground
Because the wind, seems to-
Never get tired
And moved the trees
Making the leaves sway
This way, that way all summer long
While the wind sang
A soft special song
I think the leaves are tired now
And will rest till spring
Then come in again
All dressed in green
The color scheme
Of summer
Blended with the seasons
As the seasons
Pass ageless-
As they drift with leaves
Never tired it seems,
Passing thru.

Them Beans

Them beans, them beans, the beans
That's the ones-that's talking
About where they're at.
That's what they do-
And they're good...
Very good-at it too,
Most everyone knows,
But likes them too
It seems, it seems, it seems
Them beans, the beans
Them beans.
Those powerful, powerful, powerful
Beanly-beans.

Bubbles

Today is a good day
To make bubbles
When wind is just right today,
The bubbles I make
Fly high in the air
Right over the fence
And away
Away, away, and away-
They fly
Away, away, far-rr away.

16 On

Now that you're
Almost 26 years old
And the parties-all finished
From 16 all thru-and...
Things have started
To settle
To old
And on with you-just...what
Are you going, to do
From now-thru
Just what-just what-just...
What will you do
Now, you best
Think about that
Be honest and good to you
Because if you're not there now
It comes to you
And everyone too
When the parties from 16 on
To 26 too, are finished...
And thru-what, what-just what
Will you do?

Away

There´s away-that a light
Shines thru the dark
With a glimmer
That´s meant to be seen
Like the dawn that heralds
A beautiful day.
After the storm of a night
Has faded away
And a family of light
Can love a new day
And a love that shines thru
That was thought-slipped away
But returned thru the dark
And shines forever.
Thru memory
That´s meant to be
And can be seen.
Like the dawn that heralds
The beautiful
Spiritual of day.

Dinosaurs Fly

Today...
A little boy told me
Dinosaurs fly-over the clouds
Way, up in the sky.
And that they eat small fish
When they come down too.
Also that they, like to
Go to volcanoes
To get the fire they blow it-
All over the place.
Whenever-they really want to.
That little boy told me
Lots, about dinosaurs today,
So...if
I see a dinosaur I'll sure...
Stay out of-
The dinosaurs way.

The Country

Oh the country-has a way
To hush noise and blare away
And let quiet and beauty, have its way.
For there on a hill top fair
With beauty, country beauty
All around-where
We could see, for miles-with hardly sound
And birds, sunshine, blue of sky, near
And with the creator our love, was left
Creations love-to be.
Then we left, went on our way
Together, together-and mingle
Friendly, with friends
On that same day
With plans for meeting with
And thru love-on other days.
Oh the country has a way
Of keeping love-of keeping life
All together, lovely
Quietly, beautifully...
In creations way.
And we can visit-with our friends
In the country...
Any time, at the cemetery-
They stay there, They lay there.

One Day

One day its,   today-is where
Is where our hopes
And dreams must stay
Yesterday is gone
We cannot
Bring back yesterday
Tomorrow is beyond
Our control of now
we can only plan
and this is the time
use today...
just one day,
at a time.

To Do

People kinda, after while
Get that way
So they don´t- say much
But... they, you-
Kinda push each other
Kinda out of the way
Kinda in a suttle
Kinda way.
So its soft-kinda,
Kinda like a, drifting
Cloud passed by-
Floated your way.
You can feel it
Maybe you helped too
To float that cloud by
Help it pass thru
No matter what
Its there in what's to do-
Now... kinda nudge it
In the ditch- so good
Clouds can pass thru
Cause...
People kinda after while-
Feel... that's the way
And the best thing
To do.

Difficult

The color of the blue sky
As its seen- to an individual
Appointed eye,
Is difficult- quite difficult
To match, to be
Exactly the same
On paper,
To view
As seen- as a color
"The most beautiful color"
Of the heavenly
Blue of sky
As seen- by an individuals
Appointed eye.

Me

I want to see me
Where is me
What happened to me
Where can I aim
To be the same
As before?
I want more of me
I seem to have lost me
I want to see me
Where is me
What happened
To me?

Soon

Eat tomato pie
Watch an elephant fly
See an alligator ride
A bicycle by
And watch the sun
Up high.
Also while it sets
Low in the sky.
To stand, then- soon
And say...
I've had a nice day
My friend,
Seen some of
The very best
Today-I have,
Have I...would be nice.

179

Best

Maybe
you best don't do it
if you
don't feel good
about it
because
if you, don't feel good
about it
you won't feel good
if you do
maybe-you best-do it
if you do,
your way-for you.

Birthday Party

A party, a party
A birthday party
A birthday party-for David
David's 5 years old, they say
He has a red hat on
Today.
Sitting in a chair
At the table
With children all around
Singing to the happy sound
Of happy birthday
David
Oh now... they're taking
A picture too
Of
A party, a party, a party
For David
He had a very,
Happy birthday party
And now...
Now its all thru
The party for David
David
Our, teddy bear.

Spookily Quiet

Oh so,
Spook-illy quiet
That's what it was
So quiet you could almost hear
A fly walk about
The wind was quiet
Leaves on trees were quiet
All was quiet
Even the most
Most
Of quiet ghosts
Were concerned
It was so quiet
Maybe
All noise
Had taken a vacation
A long, long vacation
And no one could scare anyone
For a long long time
That would be bad real bad
Everyone would be sad,
Real sad
It was so quiet-so...
Spook-illy quiet
That's what it was-twas so
A long long time ago.
Now...
All is ok
Noise...
Is
Here to stay.

Gifts

When we plant and sow
The creator
Makes the seed to grow
And others
Can see
The gifts-the creator
Gives thru such
As we plant and sow

A Magic

The simple slow
Of afternoon, sparks
A magic-as the day
Passes thru, a halfway-
Mark while morning
Passes to noon
And toward evening
Then twilight time.
Time it seems, is...
All the same, in
School, churches,
Everywhere, all
Working, working
As before.
Doing, doing what
Must be. Total
Total, totally.
Men, women
Children-even you,
While...
The simple plan
Of afternoon, sparks
A magic (none can stop)
As the day passes thru-
A half way mark,
While morning
Passes to noon
And toward evening
Then-twilight time.

Love

The morning sun
As it lights the sky
From morn.till noon
To the travelers eye
Is clear if clouds
Are not in view
And even then
The travelers view
From noon till night,
Thru twilight, evening,
Night, till dawn,
And morning again
Is not obscured
Even tho-
Clouds and storms,
May come.
For the traveler
Has traveled
With a faith eternal
That guides to
Creations golden
Morning sunrise.
Given thru
Faith, hope, memories
And eternal,
Love.

Doctor's Doors

The doors of
Doctors office shows feelings
As folks come
Then as they go
If opens slow- closes of fast
Maybe not so happy
As they come
If open fast- close of slow
That they may-
More of happy, go.

Stew

Alligator, and dinosaur stew
How do you make it
What do you do?
Why you just use-
Plastic alligators
And dinosaurs too
Mixed with plenty of water
That's all you have to do.
Children make it that way too
Alligator, and dinosaur stew.

Everyone

With
December almost
Finished
Just a few days
More to go
And...
Some places have
Sunshine
Some places have
Snow
But about the weather
We all know.
This, tho-
I wish for everyone
As December goes
Its way
A very merry Christmas
Happy New year too
And most lovely
Of days,
Always.

Things

Laying on your back
On the grass
You can see-just lots
And lots, and lots of things
There are to see.
Like birds flying by
The top of a tree
A leaf falling down
An airplane flying by
Maybe a bee, a fly
Or a butterfly.
Or maybe-
A dirigible too...
If it goes thru.
Oh, laying on your back
On the grass
You can see just-
Lots, and lots, and lots
Of things
There are to see.

A Greeting

A hello is a greeting
And a way to start
The day in a beautiful way
a hand shake
and a smile too
permeates thru
mixing, communicating, leading
in many ways
thru a world that
gives beauty
has hills, small, large
mountains of tall
far away close
purple with haze
with clouds, sunshine too
and also a creation
with rainbows of
colors lovely-and of
sunshine, moonlight, starlight
given freely with love
having traveled thru
this creation
witnessed the beauty
climbed the mountains-conquered
waved a victory, left memories
communicated-my way...
loved and raised a family
to friends and all, now
with my leaving
as of a sunset lovely,
consider-
a hello to evening...
and love-to sunrise.

See

I don't think-that you,
Understand my situation
Completely....
To see, also feel
How I want
To let
Things thru.
You don't-feel or see
Or see
Things finally
As me or...do you?

Late

"Watch out"....
One never knows
What its like
To be bit
By a snake
Till you're bitten.
Then as its
Written-
You'll sure know.
Course, it's-
A little late,
Then tho.

A Dreamer

Just thinking, comprehending, designing
Aware-unaware, of surroundings
In a world-
Of their own, is the dreamer.
And being in the world of..
A dreamer,
Designing how something seen-
In a dream, will be.
Later performing and assisting
In producing what he or she sees-
Is how much of what we see-
Comes to be.
From the mysteriously, interesting-
Wonderful world
Of...
A dreamer

View

For you to view-
The morning
The noon
Twilight
Evening
Night time too,
Wow...
Lucky, lucky you
You've-
Just viewed, a whole day thru
Somebody-somewhere
Really must like
You.

Songs

A November Thursday

AL VICENT

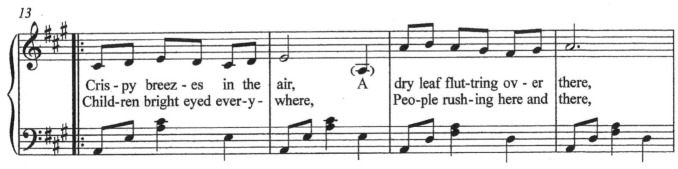

Cris - py breez - es   in the   air,   A   dry leaf flut-tring ov - er   there,
Child-ren bright eyed ever-y-   where,   Peo-ple rush-ing here and   there,

33

Peo ple thank-ful ever - y - where,
giv ing thanks in song filled ways,

For the good things that they see,
Thank ing God for watch-ful days,

37

Lets us all know in a way,
shares Love in a spe-cial way,

That it's near Thanks-giv-ing Day.
To all on Thanks-giv-ing Day.

A Nov em-ber

41

Thurs- day, A mag-i-cal Thurs-day, A thank-ful giv-ing day.

1.

2.

day.

Stories

Alfred and Rudolph's Travels

The name was Anthony P. Dragonfly and he lived at Shady Lane in a long low house, No. 116 Shady Lane Avenue, right close to a big donut house. He loved to fly early in the morning when the sun was just coming up, quiet, bright, shiny, and warm. He also especially loved to fly when the sky was blue. Anthony's very good friend was Rudolph M. Hummingbird. Rudolph lived not too far away at Crossroads Soft Moss in a small kind of rickety house with two not so tall plum trees. House No. 129 Crossroads Soft Moss Street to be exact.

Rudolph could fly really fast and almost stop anywhere. Rudolph would like to fly right after the sun was up a little bit and when the flowers were opening. He then would like to stop at lots of opening flowers and drink their sweet nectar juice. Sometimes he would meet Anthony Dragonfly and they would stop for awhile and talk because Anthony would usually be coming home from his early morning flying trip, after catching a few bugs and just exercising his wings for the day. After a short visit they usually went their different ways because Anthony Dragonfly like to skim water on the pond near his home looking for bugs and Rudolph had to hurry because he liked drinking nectar from flowers as they opened.

During their brief morning visits they became very good friends and on one visit Rudolph told Anthony Dragonfly about September each year when he always flew back to a place where the weather was warmer for the winter, then fly back here for the summer. Rudolph told Anthony it would be nice if he could go to. He might like it in the winter there. Anthony Dragonfly replied, "Yes, thank you Rudolph, but I could never fly that far or as fast as you Rudolph. I only fly close around here."

Rudolph told Anthony "I've thought about that Anthony. I've seen a train going where I fly. It blows out smoke, has a whistle, and a bell. It goes pretty fast to and stops at little towns. It has a little red car on the back. We might find nice people on the train to let us ride in the little red car, it would be nice not to have to fly. We could pack our suitcases, take some food and when the train stops, sometimes we could fly around. You find some bugs and I find some flowers with nectar, then we can get back on the train and just ride. How does that sound Anthony? I flew real close to one train. A man in the little red car saw me and said, "Oh look, a hummingbird." That man seemed nice.

Anthony said "It sounds real nice. I could not fly very far, but the train ride sounds nice. I like donuts and I could get plenty of donuts. I know some bee's that have a flower nectar shop."

"You do?" said Rudolph. "That is nice. You have a car too don't you Anthony? Why we can pick up everything and get ready. This is nice! Think about it Anthony, we can talk more about it another time. We have lots of time."

Anthony didn't waste any time, he thought about the trip! Days were nice and warm, it was summer, even the evenings were nice. They always were. Now things were a little different, since his friend Rudolph suggested they take the vacation together. Anthony always stayed close to his home before, but now he thought more about the vacation. "I'll talk to my friend Joseph Crow about our vacation plans, he always goes somewhere."

Joseph's house was not far from Anthony's place. Anthony saw Joseph outside in his yard and stopped to say, "Hello Joseph, how are you? I have not seen you for a very long time."

Joseph said "Yes I've been gone for awhile, my friends and I went up north to where the plums are getting ripe, we had a very nice time, lots of others went too. We flew but many went by train."

"Oh, is that right, by train?" said Anthony.

"Yes, by train" Joseph replied. "There's a very nice train right near here that goes most any place."

"I did not know that" Anthony replied, because Anthony always flew everywhere being a dragonfly.

"Joseph," Anthony asked, "How was your vacation? Did you have a good time?"

"Yes we did" Joseph replied. "I think everyone should take a vacation, they are nice, you can rest and see a lot of things." Joseph's friend Alfred Starling, a noisy meddlesome bird, was standing near listening, who liked to talk, spoke up and said, "Yes, I went to. We all had a nice time. I didn't fly all the way though. I rode on the train with the others."

"What is the name of this train?" Anthony asked.

"Why it's the Rabbit Choo Choo, goes all over the place here, and far far away. Bill and his cousin Jerry Rabbit drive it most of the time. Old train goes pretty fast, smokes a lot; you can see the smoke a long way off and hear the whistle."

"Thank you," Anthony replied. "Rudolph, Mr. Hummingbird, my very good friend and I are thinking about going on a vacation together. I can't fly far and fast like he does so he said it might be nice to ride a train that he had seen near here.
It must have been the Rabbit Choo Choo."

"Yes," Joseph said, "Ride the train, I think you'll like it. That must have been the Rabbit Choo Choo Rudolph saw; I think that's the only train around here close by.

Anthony told everybody "thank you, but I must go now. I have to do some work at home. Good to know vacations are nice."

Alfred Starling said loudly, "You can find the Rabbit Choo Choo station easy, at Shady Lane Avenue go to Sunrise Drive, then turn left on Sunset, fly over the hill, and you will see the station close to the bridge."

"Thank you Alfred" said Anthony.

The next day Anthony went to the train station and found out the Rabbit Choo Choo train was pretty nice. The station master told Anthony the train always had an open flat car that Anthony could put his car on. This way Anthony could use his car on his vacation then bring it back home.

The station master also told Anthony that he and Rudolph could sit in their car and ride if they wanted to. Anthony said, "my car has no top. I am so tall and my car is so small."

"That is okay" said the station master. "You can both use your parasols." Anthony was very happy and told the station master thank you and went home to tell Rudolph the good news about their vacation plans.

Rudolph was not home when Anthony got there. That was okay because, some of Anthony's friends came by. They had a good time just flying around catching a few bugs and having dragonfly races. Dragonflies can fly pretty fast Anthony thought. 'I'll have to tell my friend Rudolph he can stop over with us and maybe see how fast we fly. It was fun, lots of fun, I also saw friends I had not seen for a long time.

The next day Anthony saw Rudolph and told him about having talked to several friends and how they all had a good time on vacation. Rudolph listened as Anthony talked. When Anthony finished, Rudolph asked Anthony if he wanted to go on vacation with him. Anthony said, "Yes, I'll go. I never went on a vacation before. It sounds like fun, and the train ride with my car should be nice."

Rudolph said, "In about two more weeks I'll be ready to go. That will give us time to get everything we want to take with us ready."

September seemed to come fast this year, maybe because of the vacation they planned to take together. Anthony had his car checked to be sure it was okay and it was in good shape. The auto shop told Anthony to be sure and park the car where it would always get plenty of sunshine, because Anthony's car runs on sunshine.

Rudolph went to Anthony's place and tasted some donuts because Anthony lived by the donut shop. Anthony planned to take donuts to eat on the train, so Rudolph wanted to taste the donuts and sweet nectar from Anthony's friend's shop.

Rudolph liked the donuts, especially the plain donuts, and the chocolate flavored ones. Anthony also liked the sweet nectar from Anthony's friends shop, known as the Bee Shop.

Rudolph told Anthony to be sure and bring donuts and sweet nectar so they could eat them on the train.

Rudolph also told Anthony, "don't worry Anthony; I know plenty of places where we can find water holes with lots of bugs you can catch easy. I've seen them when I fly there all the time."

The two weeks went by real fast and Anthony Dragonfly and Rudolph Hummingbird were ready to leave on vacation. They got the tickets, loaded Anthony's car, and put the sweet nectar and donuts in Anthony's car so they could eat some anytime. The car was easy to put on the Rabbit Choo Choo flat car because Anthony just drove it up a little ramp and right on the train where it was tied down tight with special strong grape vines. The station master said at every station Anthony could drive the car off easily if he wanted.

All of Anthony and Rudolph's friends came to the train station to see their friends leave. They told them to have a nice vacation. Even Ollie Crocodile and Shorty Giraffe came.

Anthony and Rudolph climbed into Anthony's car on the Rabbit Choo Choo train. The train used sunshine for power, just like Anthony's car. It kept sunshine in a sunshine car to make the train go. Anthony's car kept sunshine in a little small box to make it run.

Anthony and Rudolph waved at their friends and away they went as the Rabbit Choo Choo train chugged off. The train rolled along, moving through the country past little houses, streams, just beautiful places.

Anthony said, "You know Rudolph, this is really nice. We just sit and it's kind of like a movie, you just watch everything. I like it. Look at those flowers, and the green grass, and the hills, and the trees. When we fly we see it too, we fly so fast we don't really think about it, but the train goes slow and we can really look at it and enjoy it more."

Rudolph answered, "Yes, I really like it; it's slow, and you can see everything. When I fly, I fly fast and stop to drink nectar from plants like those over there. Look Anthony, at that little pond over there. There must be lots of tasty bugs you could catch there. This vacation idea is really nice. I like it."

"Looking at those flowers makes me hungry" said Rudolph. "How about the nectar you brought and the donuts? Let's eat. How about you Anthony, aren't you a little hungry?"

"Yes" said Rudolph. "Let's eat. Here's the nectar Rudolph and I'll eat some donuts."

"You might like them too" said Anthony. "I just love donuts. Try some Rudolph."

"I think I will Anthony, donuts are pretty good. Next time I have flower nectar I'll come back and have a donut."

"That's good Rudolph" said Anthony, "There's plenty of donuts right here in this bag, help yourself anytime. The trains slowing down, maybe we're going to stop. "

"Oh yes, we are Rudolph" said Anthony. "This might be good because we just passed that pond where you said there might be a lot of bugs for me and plants with nectar for you. We can take off in the car and drive back there. That would be real nice."

"Hey, were going to stop and here comes Jerry Rabbit. Hi Jerry Rabbit."

"I Wonder why he's walking fast, hope everything's ok. It looks like he wants to talk with us."

"Hi Jerry" said Rudolph. "Is this a regular stop?"

"Oh yes, it is" said Jerry "I came to tell you because I remember when your car was put on the train; you said you would like to get off at long stops and take your car and look around. This is about a 2 hour stop. So take your car and have a good time. I have to get back to the engine with Bill. We're going to a little restaurant we know and it serves good fresh carrot and celery salad, makes you hungry driving this train all day. "Thanks for letting us know Jerry," said Rudolph. "Enjoy your salad at the restaurant."

"You're welcome" said Jerry. "We wanted to make sure you knew we would be here for 2 hours. Since you are out here with your car with no speaker you couldn't hear the news." Jerry then went back to work.

Anthony and Rudolph got everything ready, had gotten in the car and were about to leave, when Rudolph looked up and heard two birds calling their name.

"Anthony, Rudolph, Anthony, Rudolph!"

Rudolph said, "Anthony that looks like our friends Alfred Starling and Oscar Crow! It is our friends. I wonder what they want. Hope its good news."

When Oscar and Alfred landed they said they had chased the train for about 2 days to tell Alfred and Rudolph that Ollie Crocodile wanted them to know that his cousin Andy Alligator runs a ferry boat service at Happy Happy Lake Resort.

"It goes around the resort on the lake over to Flower Bug Island," Ollie said, "It's a really nice place and so is the island, so stop there if you can and be sure to tell Andy Alligator hi from Ollie Crocodile, his cousin. We must go now Anthony and Rudolph. Have a nice vacation. Glad we caught up to you vacation travelers."

"Thank you Oscar and Alfred. We'll stop there, please tell Ollie thank you and have a good time flying back home" said Rudolph.

When they left, Anthony told Rudolph that it was nice Oscar and Alfred flew so far to bring them that information and good that Ollie Crocodile remembered they were on vacation. "We will enjoy Happy Happy Resort so we must stop there and see Ollie's cousin, Andy Alligator," said Anthony.

"Of course," said Rudolph "We have to do that."

Then Anthony drove off the train flat car and he and Rudolph were off to look at the little town. As they drove along Anthony saw a sign, "SEE A DEEPY CREEPY CAVE."

Anthony asked Rudolph, "Rudolph did you see that sign?"

"Yes," Rudolph answered "I saw it. Let's stop and take a look."

Anthony stopped the car, both got out and walked to the office. A large beaver named Tom worked there and told them, "Hi I'm Tom Beaver, can I help you?"

Rudolph said, "We would like to visit the Deepy Creepy Cave!"

"Ok," said Tom Beaver, "Its free today. Terry Turtle will take you through."

Tom called Terry the Turtle. Terry came over and said "Climb on my back."

Tom gave Anthony and Rudolph two lanterns with fireflies inside.

"When it's dark in the cave the fireflies will give light and you can see. Hang on to the lanterns," Said Tom.

"Ok" Anthony and Rudolph said.

Then Terry started walking up a little path through some bushes and into the cave. Terry kept walking. The path went down, down, down. Deeper, deeper, deeper till they were down very, very, very deep. The fireflies made the lanterns nice and bright so Anthony and Rudolph could see ok.

Then one of the fireflies said, "I'm tired, I'm going to rest" and the lanterns went out. All the fireflies went to sleep, and it got very dark. Terry Turtle hollered at the fireflies, "Hey you guys wake up!," but all the fireflies were asleep.

Terry said, "That's okay, I know the way." Then suddenly, Terry yelled, "Hang on tight guys, its wet here. We're going to slide a long way. They slid for a long, long way, always deeper, deeper, deeper in the cave. They suddenly bumped into something and stopped. Terry started walking again and said, "You guys okay?" Anthony and Rudolph said, "We're okay; how about you Terry?"

Terry replied, "I'm okay, I kind of liked the slide. Did you keep the lanterns?"

Anthony and Rudolph said, "Yes, we did"

Terry said, "That's good; those fireflies will probably wake up soon and give us some light. Oh yes, pretty soon you may hear some strange noises. I know it's very dark with no lanterns, but don't be too afraid. No one has ever been hurt yet, but we don't know what or who makes the noise when we walk by."

For a very long time, Anthony and Rudolph heard a noise like someone was walking close behind Terry. Then, all of a sudden, Anthony and Rudolph heard the noise turn and go the other way. It was very scary.

Then they heard a scraping noise like someone was scraping a cake pan. It kept going on for a long time. Then, a dragging sound, like someone was dragging a big bag or something for a long time.

Then all of the noise stopped!

All the time, Terry kept walking deeper, deeper, deeper into the cave. It was very dark too, because all the fireflies were resting, and there was no light.

Terry asked, "You guys okay? Did you hear all the noises?"

Anthony and Rudolph said, "Yes we did, and it was very scary."

"I know; we don't know who makes the noises. They seem to like to do that, but they never hurt anybody. Hang on, you'll like the next part," said Terry.

197

About the time Terry the Turtle finished talking, a large pair of hands picked up Terry, Anthony, and Rudolph. You could hear feet running, but could not hear anyone breathing, just the hands holding Terry the Turtle, Anthony, and Rudolph. They also felt wind and soft noise like wings flapping. It felt good. And very soon they were back almost at the entrance of the cave where Terry had started their adventure. It was still too dark to see.

Then the hands set everybody down and you could hear the sound of footsteps walking away. The fireflies soon awakened and said "We're all rested now" and gave a good light.

Terry listened and told the fireflies, "Next time, don't do that. We needed light in the cave."

The fireflies said, "Sorry, but we were tired."

Terry asked Anthony and Rudolph, "How did you like Deepy Creepy Cave?" Anthony and Rudolph both said that it was good, but scary too.

Terry kept walking. Soon they were out in the sunlight and saw Tom Beaver who also asked them how they liked Deepy Creepy Cave, both told Tom it was good fun. They needed to get back to the train so they told everybody thank you, got in Anthony's car, said goodbye, and left.

Rudolph said, "Anthony, we'd better go back to the train. It's getting late, and we only could stay for two hours. We'd better hurry." Anthony drove pretty fast, and when they got there, the train was waiting.

Anthony drove onto the flat car, tied his car down with the grape vine, and soon the Rabbit Choo Choo was moving again.

It was a nice day; the train moved along very nicely. Rudolph and Anthony were tired from their visit in the cave, so they rested and slept for a little while, in fact almost two hours. When Rudolph awakened, he noticed the train was going up a pretty big hill. Rudolph wanted Anthony to see the hills too because there were no big hills where Anthony lived. So Rudolph awakened Anthony, all the time saying, "Look, look Anthony! We are in the hill area, big big hills."

"Anthony I usually fly over these hills when I go to my place in the winter and I never really pay much attention to these hills. But to see them from a train, they are beautiful. What do you think of the hill's Anthony?"

Anthony kept looking. He never saw anything like this before and he told Rudolph, "I have never seen big hills before. This is just beautiful. I'll have to tell Alfred Starling and Oscar Crow about this so they can come see this sometime too."

The Rabbit Choo Choo kept going up,up,up in the hills. Anthony and Rudolph just looked. Anthony did not know what to say, so he said nothing, he just looked and looked at the hills. Then he saw something really different. The ground all covered with white and he said, "Rudolph! Rudolph! What is that white stuff all over the ground on the hills over there?"

Rudolph said, "Oh that? That is snow."

Anthony said, "I have never seen snow, I hope the train stops somewhere near here for a little while so we can go over and look at snow. It is pretty to see. I have never seen anything like that before. "

"I fly this way sometime" said Rudolph. "On the other side of this mountain there is no snow, it's only on the top. I can't fly that high. I don't fly that high but I see the snow when I pass here. Pretty soon we will be where I stay for the winter."

While Rudolph was talking Bill, one of the engineers, came and told Anthony, "Hi, Jerry, and I drive the train. I was just checking the train, just passing through, not much to talk about. Keep doing everything the same."

"Nice trip so far, everything ok here," said Anthony.

"Yes" Bill told them. "We'll be stopping soon at Chilly Station. Be there for 3 hours. Engine needs more sunshine. It was hard pulling coming up the hillside. You might want to take your car and drive around a little when we stop at Chilly Station. If you go to the mountain be careful in the snow. It's different to drive in and it will be cold there too. Do you have jackets?"

Anthony and Rudolph asked each other about jackets and remembered they had put jackets in their bags. So they told Bill the train driver, "Thank you for reminding them about the jackets, they will remember to take jackets with them when they leave to go see the snow."

Bill replied, "You are very welcome, I must go now. We are getting near Chilly Station and Jerry needs me to help, especially since we are in the mountains. I just put speakers in your car. Now you can hear all the announcements too."

"Thank you" said Anthony.

Soon Anthony and Rudolph could feel the train slowing down and heard over the speakers, "Next stop Chilly Station. We will be there for 3 hours. We will be there for 3 hours. We will be there for 3 hours! The engine needs more sunshine. We are using more sunshine pulling in the mountains, our fuel is low. Next stop Chilly Station!"

When the train stopped at Chilly Station, Anthony and Rudolph quickly took off the strong grapevine tied to Anthony's car, got in and drove off the train's flatcar on to the platform which leads down to the street. They were now off to see snow.

Anthony and Rudolph had never seen snow before. "Rudolph," Anthony said "we must stop and put on our jackets; I'm getting cold."

"Yes, and so am I" said Rudolph. "Let's put on our jackets." After they put on their jackets, Rudolph said "These jackets feel good; let's go see the snow Anthony."

Anthony drove on and they saw some deer by the roadside. The mother deer had some babies and they noticed the father deer looked up as they approached.

Anthony stopped and said, "Hello everyone. We are off to see the snow."

Father deer said "That is nice. The snow is beautiful, but be careful; the snow is slippery."

"We will," said Anthony.

Anthony told the deer family thank you and goodbye and drove on. Soon they passed a family of friends eating. Some partridges, doves, and blue jays were talking and having a good time.

Anthony stopped and told them, "We are going to see the snow."

The doves told Anthony and Rudolph, "That is nice; have a good time with the weather. This is the Hoppity Mountain Range. The snow is mostly on the Great Hoppity mountains, so be careful!" The partridges and blue jays also said to be careful.

Anthony and Rudolph thanked everybody, waved, and drove on. Soon they came to the snow. Anthony told Rudolph, "It's beautiful over here; we are almost to the top. The road is pretty good." Soon they saw a mountain goat but Anthony didn't stop. As he approached, he blew the horn and waved as he slowed the car down to say, "Hello, we are looking at the snow."

The mountain goat said, "Have a good time," as Anthony drove on.

Then Rudolph said, "Look at the beautiful trees and everything we can see far from here. Oh look Anthony, that sign says top of Hoppity Mountain. Let's turn back." Anthony started to turn around in a bad place, because under the snow was some ice which caqused the car slid into some bushes and get stuck in the snow. The wheels just spun in the snow.

Anthony said, "Rudolph, we are stuck. What will we do? We only had three hours before the train was leaving …we only have about an hour left."

About that time, a friendly squirrel in a nearby tree eating acorns he saved from the summer was watching from his tree house. He hollered down, "Hello, I'm Jimminy Squirrel; could I come help in any way?"

"Yes you could, I'm Anthony P. Dragonfly and my friend here is Rudolph M. Hummingbird, were just passing by on the Rabbit Choo Choo Train with our car. The train stopped, and we are driving around looking at the beautiful Hoppity Mountains, and now we're stuck in the snow. We would be very happy if you could give us a push."

Jimminy Squirrel said, "I would be happy to do that, and I'll bring my friend Quickly Rat with me, since he's visiting with me today. We'll be right down. Come on Quickly, let's go!"

"Okay," said Quickly, he had been listening and watching too. Soon they were down and pushed Anthony's car out of the snow. Anthony gave them each a donut with a little flower nectar that Anthony had in the car. They said thank you, waved goodbye, and Anthony and Rudolph were on their way back down Hoppity Mountain.

The car went down the mountain quite fast and they passed everybody that they had seen coming up the mountain. They blew their horn and waved as they said goodbye. Soon they were back to Chilly Station and drove their car up the ramp back onto the flatcar, tied it down with the strong grapevine, and the Rabbit Choo Choo was moving again.

Anthony and Rudolph said, "that was nice; I enjoyed seeing Hoppity Mountain and the Hoppity Mountain Range. They were beautiful, and everyone we met there was nice. I think the next stop will be Happy Happy Lake Resort where Andy Alligator, Ollie Crocodile's cousin, works. I think the train stays there for about three days. If it does, that will be good because we can have Andy Alligator take us to the Flower Bug Island that we have heard so much about since he runs a ferry service there."

"Yes, that will be great" said Rudolph. "I'm glad you remembered. We *must* see that island."

"Anthony," Rudolph said, "It won't be long after we leave Happy Happy Lake Resort before we get to the place where I stay all winter."

"That will be so nice Rudolph, I can hardly wait. This has been a very nice trip so far and I have really enjoyed the train ride. This is the first time I ever rode on a train and the Rabbit Choo Choo, is so nice. The dining car is so nice too."

"Yes," said Rudolph, "The carrot celery soup we had today was delicious."

"It really was," said Anthony. "Those Red Squirrels that do most of the cooking are good cooks."

"Anthony, isn't the train going very slowly? Say, we just stopped. Why, I wonder why! There is no station here. *Why did we stop?*"

"I don't know Rudolph" Anthony answered.

About that time, an announcement came over the train speaker system. "The train has been held up by the Rabbit Cowboys. They are fox-riding cowboys; you may see some of the cowboys near your car wandering around. I will put the leader on the speaker system, he wants to say something."

"Hello everybody, my name is Hector and I'm the leader of the Rabbit Cowboys. We held up your train because we want your carrot celery soup! We have brought our soup tank wagon, so this won't take long and we'll be gone if your cooks cooperate and give us the soup with no trouble."

"We know you have the soup because our look-out Rabbits have been sniffing and know you're cooking carrot celery soup on this train and we want some, but not all. We will leave you enough to get to Happy Happy Lake Resort, but no more."

Anthony said, "Oh, look over there Rudolph at the foxes pulling that wagon with the rabbit driving. That must be the tank wagon the leader talked about."

"Yes Anthony, I think it is" said Rudolph.

Then, Hector came back on the speaker system and said, "Thank you for the soup. Goodbye." And the Rabbit Choo Choo started moving again.

Anthony said, "Rudolph I think that's terrible. Those cowboy bandits should be stopped. I'll tell my friend Ernie Eagle about this, he goes fishing at the little lake near here all the time. The nerve of those Cowboy Rabbits to hold up this train."

"You know Rudolph, I just got a good idea. Your friend Ernie Eagle flies really high and really quiet and he can see a long way. Maybe he could watch the Rabbit Choo Choo sometimes and when these Rabbit Cowboys come by to rob the train, he could swoop down, pick up a cowboy, and drop the cowboy in the water at the Happy Happy Lake Resort; which is close to here."

"Yes Anthony, that's a good idea. It would serve those Rabbit Cowboys right" said Rudolph.

"The next time I see Ernie Eagle I'll ask him if he will do that. He will probably laugh and say, "Of course I will, that will be fun to do. Ernie's a good friend and he will be glad to help" said Rudolph.

"Oh yes Anthony, did you notice each Rabbit Cowboy had a bow and arrow on his shoulder?"

"No, I didn't notice that Rudolph."

"I did" said Rudolph.

"Those Rabbit Cowboys really wanted that soup. Maybe they are sitting around a big campfire, eating their stolen carrot celery soup right now" said Anthony.

And that is just what they were doing, keeping all the other animals close by grumbling, awake, and angry. But the Rabbit Cowboys didn't care. They told the other animals 'Oh be quiet, we don't care; we are having fun."

The train moved along slowly, but nice and smooth. Anthony and Rudolph just looked at the country pass by as the train moved.

Then Rudolph said, "Anthony, I fly this way sometimes but there is not too much out here other than some rabbits, squirrels and birds."

Anthony replied, "Yes, it looks pretty quiet out here."

About that time, the train started to slow some more and the conductor came over the speaker saying, "Next stop will be Happy Happy Lake Resort. We will be here for three days."

When the train stopped Anthony told Rudolph, "Let's go to the room that I made a reservation for. We can rest tonight and find Andy Alligator, Ollie Crocodile's cousin, tomorrow. Then we can catch his ferry to Flower Bug Island and stay there for two days before returning to the train and then it's off to your winter rest place at Nicely Nice Winter Rest."

After a very good night's rest, Anthony woke up first then woke up Rudolph. "Rudolph, let's go eat. I'm hungry. I saw a nice breakfast pond on one side and flowers with nectar on the other side. I'll eat on the pond side and you can find nectar on the other side. Let's meet here when we finish and go find Andy Alligator, Ollie's cousin, and catch the ferry to Flower Bug Island."

"Sounds like a good idea" said Rudolph. "Let's go eat breakfast; I'm hungry too."

Rudolph finished eating first and waited just a little while for Anthony to return. "Anthony," Rudolph said, "How was breakfast?"

Anthony said, "Very good, the pond had lots of bugs. How was your breakfast?"

"Good, good, I mean very good too. The flowers had lots of nectar. This place has lots of good things to eat. Now let's go find Andy Alligator and his ferry service to Flower Bug Island."

As they headed for the ferry boat, they saw a kangaroo hopping along, so they flew low and asked the kangaroo about Andy Alligator's ferry boat service.

"Oh yes," the kangaroo replied, "I'm Kindy Kangaroo, and I work there. It's about six good hops away…follow me!"

They were soon at the ferry boat office where Andy was sitting outside in the sunshine waiting for customers. Rudolph and Anthony went right over, met Andy Alligator, and told him they were Ollie Crocodile's friends. They said Ollie had told them to look Andy his cousin the ferry boat operator up and tell him hello and be sure to visit Flower Bug Island.

Andy said, "Thank you, and when you go back tell Ollie hello from me, Andy Alligator."

"We'll do that," said Rudolph and Anthony.

"Now," Andy said, "Let me take you to Bus Island. Are you ready?"

"Yes, let's go" Rudolph and Anthony replied.

"Follow me" said Andy. "See that big log in the water? Hop on and I'll push you to Flower Bug Island. That log is the ferry." With Andy pushing, soon they were at Flower Bug Island.

"Here we are" said Andy. "There is a lot to see here and plenty to eat. There are lots of bugs, flowers with delicious nectar, beautiful sunrises and sunsets to see, fish swimming by, even an old shipwreck on the other side of the island that's been there for years.

"There is also a little train that runs around the island. It's free, everything at Happy Happy Resort is free, like the Rabbit Choo Choo. Everything is free; it all comes from sunshine kept in big sunshine tanks.

"Enjoy everything, be careful, and have fun."

"See you in two days. Thank you and bye" Anthony and Rudolph told Andy.

Anthony left his car on the train because it would be too much trouble to take to Flower Bug Island on the ferry, so they walked a little and looked at the island. Then the island train came.

"Let's catch the train and look at the island" said Rudolph.

"Yes" said Anthony, "That's the best way to see it."

"This is a pretty big island" said Anthony. "What is that big building over there? It looks empty." The train driver heard Anthony and said, "This island, a very long time ago, was kept by a lot of pirates. They made the buildings."

A red squirrel was driving the little train and said, "People never come here." The driver kept talking and said, "Sometimes when you look at the old buildings you can see people, but when you go over there, nobody is there. Over there, see the seals playing and laying in the sun? There are lots of fish on this side jumping, playing, and eating. Sometimes our friend Ernie the Eagle comes here and fishes. He's very nice. Everybody likes Ernie."

Rudolph said, "Ernie, he's my friend too, I've known Ernie a long time. Anthony and I were just talking about him yesterday when the Rabbit Cowboys held up the train for carrot celery soup. We were saying it would be nice if Ernie could catch one of those bandit cowboys and drop him in the lake. Wouldn't that be nice?"

"Oh yes" the driver said "There is always talk about those Rabbit Cowboys. They are quite a bunch of bad guys."

Rudolph said, "I hope we get to see Ernie while we're here or at Nicely Nice Winter Rest. That's where were going. That's the next stop I think."

"Yes it is" said the driver. "I'm sure you'll see Ernie. He comes around here all the time. Since this is your first visit to Flower Bug Island and it's early in the morning, I'm in no big hurry."

The driver said "I'll just point out some of the things to see. You can come back and look at them if you stay for 1 or two days."

"We'll be here for two days," said Anthony.

As the train moved along, on the left side was Lookout Mountain, from there you can see over most of the island. "You can see where the seals and fish play. All over the island, there are lot s of bugs and many beautiful flowers. As we move along you can see that old building. It's called the Old Castle. It's empty, but since you guys can fly you can fly over and look in it. That should be fun. Oh by the way everyone just calls me Red. I'm from the Red Squirrel Family," the driver said.

"Thank you" said Rudolph, "My name is Rudolph and my friends name is Anthony. Thank you Red for showing us so many interesting things to see."

"I have told you about most of the things to seen on Flower Bug Island but you have to see the Twilight Rainbow before you leave. You must be close to the Old Castle building to see it and if you look down near the beach when the Twilight Rainbow comes, the mermaids will come out to watch the rainbow. That is the only time you ever see the mermaids when the rainbow finishes they stay a little while and then go back into the water."

"We must see the Twilight Rainbow before we leave," said Anthony.

"There's a little place near the castle you might want to stay the night at since there are lots of flowers and bugs. Anywhere in this place there isn't a bad spot to watch the Twilight Rainbow but two days will go fast. You can take your time, fly around and I will be close by with the train when you are ready to leave."

"Thank you Red, we'll do that," said Anthony.

"Sounds good Rudolph"

"Thanks Red"

Red left with the train. Anthony and Rudolph found the place near the castle that Red spoke of. Rudolph had lots of flower nectar and Anthony had a lot of bugs. They rested and then flew around and came back to the old castle. Both days they watched the Twilight Rainbow and the mermaids. The mermaids watched Anthony and Rudolph as they all watched the Twilight Rainbow together. Then the mermaids would play a little in the water near the beach and go back into the water.

The mermaids had long black hair and faces and arms like people. They lived in the water near the old castle. Anthony and Rudolph had never seen them anywhere else. Rudolph and Anthony spent two days on Flower Bug Island but came back each day to the rest area by the old castle to watch the Twilight Rainbow with the mermaids. They thought they saw people near the castle but never did even though Rudolph could fly and stand still in the air. As he flew, he would stop in mid-air and look into the old castle windows. The beds were all made up nice like someone was there but they never saw anyone. I was the same with the old ship wreck, no one was around.

Anthony and Rudolph flew and rode the train all over the island and had a good time. They thanked the island train driver Red, and said, "We enjoyed the visit especially the Twilight Rainbow and the strange visit with the castle mermaids."

Then they went to the ferry place and Andy Alligator was waiting with his ferry. He asked them if they enjoyed the visit on Flower Bug Island. Anthony and Rudolph told Andy thank you and the visit to Flower Bug Island was very nice.

Soon they were back to Happy Happy Lake Resort and told Andy Alligator thank you and that they would tell Ollie Crocodile hello from Andy Alligator. Then they got back on the Rabbit Choo Choo and continued on their way to Nicely Nicely Winter Rest. The three day stop over at Happy Happy Lake Resort was nice. Everyone had a nice rest and looked forward to the rest of the trip to Nicely Nicely Winter Rest.

After the Rabbit Choo Choo Train traveled around huge Happy Happy Lake and got out of the Hoppity Mountain Range, everything was nice.

Rudolph said, "Anthony this is where a lot of my eagle friends live. I think this is where Ernie is from. I do hope we get to see Ernie while we are here this winter."

Anthony answered "I certainly want to meet Ernie, I'm sure we will."

"Anthony" Rudolph said "I know this place very well, because I come here every winter. We will be there soon. It's not far after we leave Happy Happy Lake Resort. I'm sure you will like Nicely Nicely Winter Rest. Most everyone comes here for winter"

Then the Rabbit Choo Choo started to slow and the conductor said "Next stop Nicely Nicely Winter Rest."

When the train stopped, Anthony and Rudolph removed the very strong grapevine holding Anthony's car down and carefully drove off the ramp. Rudolph showed Anthony where to go for their winter vacation place, Nicely Nicely Winter Rest.

"Drive this way" Rudolph told Anthony. "Turn at the next corner. Keep going straight till I tell you to stop."

"Alright" Anthony said.

They had not gone too far when Rudolph said, "This big lake we are passing is Lake Nicely. Lots of my good friends live here. There's Rupert Bullfrog, Homer Cricket, Tony Turtle, and of course my long time friend Mr. Willie Skunk and Kathy Katydid."

"At the next corner turn left Anthony."

"Ok," said Rudolph turning before he forgot.

"Rudolph you have lots of friends here?"

"Oh yes," said Rudolph "I've been coming here for a long time."

"That's nice," said Anthony.

"Thank you Anthony, I'm sure you will meet a lot of new friends here also, seems everyone does. This big place on the right side is a big open hotel where everybody stays. It's all free. All you have to do is use plenty of sunshine every day. If you have cars or anything like that, keep it filled all the time and use plenty of sunshine. If you don't your friends are supposed to check on you and find out why. So remember Anthony, use plenty of sunshine and keep your car filled with sunshine everyday so you and your car are ready to go anytime. Remember everything is free. "

At just about twilight, right before evening every night, "The choir starts singing. Almost everybody and anybody can sing and everyone wants you to sing as long as you want. I know my friends all sing except Willie Skunk. I don't think I have ever heard him sing," said Rudolph.

"We can park your car almost anywhere since there's not many cars here, most just fly in or catch the Rabbit Choo Choo."

"Oh there's a different car. I have never seen that one before. That's Rupert Bullfrog. He sings base in the choir at night. I must tell him hello" said Rudolph "This is the first time I have seen him on this visit."

"Hello Rupert," said Rudolph "Good to see you."

"Good to see you too Rudolph."

"This is my friend Anthony. He came with me for vacation this time. Anthony this is Rupert," said Rudolph. They exchange greetings of nice to meet each other.

"We came on the Rabbit Choo Choo train. It was a nice ride," said Anthony.

"Where did you get the car Rupert?" said Rudolph.

"Oh," said Rupert "a friend gave it to me. He drove it down from somewhere, got tired of it and I've been using it. I used to come on the train all the time too but I will probably take my car back this time though. You two could ride back too if you want to send your car back by train. It's all free."

"We'll think about it. Thanks Rupert. Nice to see you again Rupert," said Rudolph.

"Same here," said Rupert, "And nice to meet you Anthony."

"Nice to meet you too Rupert," said Anthony.

"Oh say Rupert," said Rudolph "Have you seen Ernie Eagle?"

"Yes I did," said Rupert "I saw him yesterday. He was fishing in the lake near me. He landed and I swam over and we talked for a long time. In fact we talked about you. I wondered when you would get here on vacation."

"That's nice," said Rudolph. "When you see him again tell him hello and that we're here and would like to see him."

"I'll do that," said Rupert. "Bye."

Then Rudolph and Anthony flew down a couple of blocks. Rudolph pointed out a place filled with lots of bugs.

"This is another one of our outdoor restaurants. There are several of these so you can eat anytime you want too."

"Let's just fly around some and look at the place," said Rudolph. "It's a pretty big place and the weather here is nice too. It is a very nice place for the winter. Say, that must be Ernie over there. Let's fly by and tell him hello," said Rudolph, "And I can introduce you to Ernie."

"Let's do that," said Rudolph.

When they got over where Ernie was sitting, Ernie was surprised and said, "Hi Rudolph, Rupert Bullfrog and I were talking about you the other day and wondering when you would get here."

"Well here we are Ernie. This is my friend Anthony Dragonfly. I invited him to come on vacation. Anthony this is Ernie Eagle."

Ernie and Anthony exchanged greetings of "nice to meet you." Then Rudolph told Ernie it took them a little longer because they rode the Rabbit Choo Choo train.

"Oh that's nice," said Ernie. "I see it a lot. Rupert Bullfrog said he rides it too sometimes."

"Yes he told us yesterday when we saw him. He said he rides it sometimes but yesterday he was driving a car. He said his friend had given him the car," said Rudolph.

Ernie sai,d "Oh yes he does drive the car. I can't ride in his car. It's too small for me, I'd rather fly anyway. I like to fly high and see everything."

"Oh Ernie, there was something I wanted to tell you. When we came on the Rabbit Choo Choo near Happy Happy Lake Resort those pesky Rabbit Cowboys held up the train and stole some of the carrot celery soup. I was thinking, it would be nice if sometime you were flying by that way if you could kind of keep watch from above. If you see those cowboys robbing the train riding foxes and using them to pull their wagon that carries the carrot celery soup they steal, we thought maybe you could swoop down, pick up one of the cowboys, fly over Happy Happy Lake Resort and drop him in the lake. Serve him right. He could swim out all wet and walk home. What do you think about that Ernie?"

Ernie said, "Rudolph that sounds like great fun. I'd just love to do that. I catch fish like that all the time. I've never caught a Rabbit Cowboy like that before but it would be easier than catching a fish. And then to carry him high in the air and drop him in the lake wow, that would just be lots of vacation fun. Why don't both of you hop on? Let's go take a little fly around the place. I'm sure we can find out where those cowboys stay. I've heard about them and we can see the entire vacation place too. You guys hang on good though. Kind of stick your feet under my feathers and hang on."

Ernie spread his big wings and away they went. Ernie flew real high then he called back to Anthony and Rudolph, "Everything ok back there?"

"Everything's fine" said Anthony and Rudolph, "We're just enjoying the ride. You could fly a little lower and then we can see better."

"Ok" said Ernie "I'm used to flying high but I'll just spread my wings and not flap them so much and glide around up here. Have a good time. Maybe we can see the Rabbit Choo

Choo train and maybe those Rabbit Cowboys will be around too. If they are bothering the train I'll glide down real quiet, pick up the bad guy, drop him in the water over in the Happy Happy Lake and you guys can watch."

"Sounds like fun. I'd really like to do that. Let's go see if we can find the Rabbit Choo Choo and see if everything is ok."

"Yes let's go," said Anthony and Rudolph.

"Ok," said Ernie "We'll keep gliding around and I'll keep looking and see if we can find the train and if it's ok."

Ernie circled around gracefully. "Look at the Nicely Nice Winter Rest. It's really a nice place with lots of flowery wet places. There are a lot of nice and quiet looking restful places. It really looks nice. I think you will like it here Anthony. You should have a nice relaxing vacation. We like it here don't we Rudolph?" said Ernie.

"I think it is too. I certainly got a nice look at the whole place looking down while you circled over from high in the sky. It looks nice and thank you Ernie," said Anthony.

Oh look at what I just saw. The Rabbit Choo Choo train and it's stopped way out here. There's no station or anything out there. Let's go down and see if everything is ok," said Ernie.

"I can see what is wrong now" said Ernie "The Rabbit Cowboys have held up the train again. I can see them walking around. They use foxes to ride on."

"Just hang on tight now, Rudolph your idea of picking up a cowboy and dropping him in the water, I think I can do that easy now because I fish like this all the time. I can see from here. My eyes help me catch fish all the time. Just hang on tight both of you here we go."

Ernie dived quickly and picked up the cowboy by his loose fitting clothes and carried him over to Happy Happy Lake and dropped him in the lake. It happened so quiet and quick that the other cowboys did not know at first what to do. Then they quickly ran away.

When Ernie, Rudolph, and Anthony came back the train had started to move again but Ernie flew a little lower and the train engineer waved and hollered, "Thank you" to Ernie.

Ernie told Rudolph, "Your idea worked well. We really surprised those cowboys. I hope I did not hurt the cowboy. My claws are very strong. I tried to catch just his clothes to pick him up and carry him to the lake. He sure looked surprised when he was falling into the water. It will be something the cowboys and the train riders can talk about for a long time. It was fun too."

"It really was," said Rudolph "and thank you Ernie. I'm happy Anthony and I were with you to see you do this."

"Thank you," said Ernie.

Ernie, Rudolph, and Anthony flew around Nicely Nicely Winter Rest looking the place over a little more then Ernie landed where he first picked his friends up.

Rudolph and Anthony told Ernie thank you and Ernie said, "I'll go rest now too. This has been fun. See you both again later."

And Anthony and Rudolph agreed that was a nice ride. They also talked about how surprised that cowboy must have been to be picked up and dropped in Happy Happy Lake. Then they ate and rested at the Nicely Nice Open Hotel. They stayed close by for a few weeks having a good time because they were on vacation.

One morning after eating a good breakfast of bugs and most delicious flower nectar at the Open Hotel Restaurant, Anthony and Rudolph were just flying around when Anthony said,

"Look Rudolph isn't that Hasty and Marie snail over there coming this way?"

Rudolph said, "Yes Anthony that does look like them. Let's go over and say hello."

When they got there it was Hasty and Marie. Rudolph and Anthony told them both hello and asked how they came. Hasty and Marie told them they came on the Rabbit Choo Choo and that it was a nce trip all the way, no trouble at all.

"We certainly had a nice ride. That's nice Anthony answered we came on the Rabbit Choo Choo too. Enjoy your visit this is a nice place."

Many of Rudolph and Anthony's friends kept coming to Nicely Nice Winter Rest. Rudolph and Anthony had been there for a long time and Rudolph told Anthony "It's time to go back to the Very Best Summer Place now. We better leave soon and tell our friends we are leaving. It's been nice here for the winter. Hope you had a nice time Anthony."

"Oh yes it was very nice. Thank you for inviting me Rudolph."

About that time Rupert Bullfrog drove by in his car and said "Hi Rudolph and Anthony haven't seen you in awhile. How is everything?"

"Oh, were ok," said Anthony and Rudolph "We're thinking of going back to Very Best Summer Place soon. We have been here for the winter. It's time to go back now."

"You know," said Rupert "I'm going back soon too. Would you like to ride back in my car? It's pretty big. It has two seats in back you could each have a seat.

"Anthony you could send your car back on the train? The road is pretty close to the Rabbit Choo Choo track. You could see your car most of the time."

"Think about it. If you want to ride with me we can leave anytime you want to go. I'm going for a swim at that little lake right over there. Think about it. Let me know, we could all ride back together."

Anthony and Rudolph thought about it, talked about it, and decided to ship Rudolph's little car back on the Rabbit Choo Choo and ride back with Rupert Bullfrog in his car. The three decided to leave together, so the next morning, right after the sun came up, they put everything in Rupert's big car. They packed their bags with some donuts, Anthony liked donuts, some sweet flower nectar for Rudolph and bugs for Rupert, Anthony also liked bugs with his donuts. They also packed their jackets. Rupert had a jacket made of yellow duck feathers and said he wanted to see the snow in Hoppity Mountains. He heard about the snow but never seen it before. Rupert always wore a cowboy hat when he drove his big car. Anthony asked Rupert if he had had his car checked and Rupert said he has filled it with sunshine for the trip back.

Rupert said, "Yes, everything ok."

So everybody hopped in and zoomed away. They went in Rupert's big car with Rupert driving, Anthony in the middle seat and Rudolph in the back seat. On their way back to the Very Best Summer Rest from Nicely Nice Winter Rest, they planned to stop at the Happy Happy Lake Resort to visit Flower Bug Island because Rupert Bullfrog had heard about the old buildings on Flower Bug Island and the Twilight Rainbow and the mermaids that come to watch it each evening.

With his heavy bullfrog voice and wearing his cowboy hat, Rupert said, "I have never seen a mermaid, I want to see a mermaid, I heard they're very beautiful." Rupert likes cowboy hats. Everything went nice. Rupert liked to drive fast. The road back was pretty close to the track the Rabbit Choo Choo traveled on.

Rupert reminded Anthony, "See Anthony we will be able to see your car on the train.

The train left for Very Best Summer Rest not too long ago. We will probably see it pretty soon."

They had traveled not too far away when they saw the train. It was moving along pretty fast. Anthony and Rudolph could see their friend Bill Rabbit driving. He had his arm out the engine window and he could see his brother Jerry Rabbit sitting on the other side. They could also smell the carrot celery soup and other tasty food being cooked in the train kitchen. Anthony and Rudolph waved at Bill Rabbit and he waved back. Rupert Bullfrog waved too.

Rupert asked, "You know the driver?"

"Yes," Rudolph said "They are our friends. We know Bill and Jerry from Nicely Nice Summer Rest."

"Oh," said Rupert, "That's nice."

"That soup sure smelled good," said Anthony.

"Yes it did," said Rupert and Rudolph. "They have good cooks on the train."

Then the road came to a sharp turn. So did the railroad. The train stopped and the engine turned over, and so did most of the cars. Rupert stopped right away, because the road was close to the railroad track at that place too.

When Rupert, Anthony, and Rudolph got there, they could see a large tree had fallen across the railroad track. Bill and Jerry did not see the tree in time to stop the train so the train hit the tree and turned over.

They could see Bill and Jerry, they seemed okay. They could hear Bill say very loudly to Jerry, "TURN OFF THE SUNSHINE. DON'T LOSE THE SUNSHINE."

"I did," said Jerry.

The kitchen car was almost to the back of the train near the Little Red Caboose and it did not turn over. Rudolph and Anthony were flying around together and Rudolph was watching near the engine. Anthony heard the cooks say, "cover the soup so it doesn't spill."

Then Rudolph said, "Look Anthony, that eagle that just landed looks like Ernie. Let's go see if that is Ernie." They both went over and spoke to Ernie. Ernie said he had gotten up early, was just flying around, saw the Rabbit Choo Choo, saw it turn over, and came to see if he could help.

Ernie said he had seen a few animals together not too far away. He would go ask them if maybe they wanted to help. "Do you want to go?" asked Ernie. Rudolph had already introduced Rupert the Bullfrog to Ernie. Ernie said "You three want to go? Hop on; I feel strong this morning. Hang on, here we go!"

Rupert said, "This is nice; I have never flown before. There are the animals in that big group over there."

"Some kind of meeting I think" said Ernie. "I'll land and we will tell them about the train wreck."

Ernie landed and told them about the train wreck. The animals all thanked Ernie, Alfred, Rudolph, and Rupert, and said they would go right over because the railroad was close by. There was Elley Elephant and his friend Bob Elephant that just happened to be visiting and had found the group of early morning risers for a meeting. Everyone came together and was happy for the nice weather with sunshine and a very nice spring season. Then they planned to go to Nicely Nice Winter Rest Hotel Open Restaurant and vacation for a few days. But now they will hurry over and help with the train wreck. Ernie and his friends thanked everyone. Anthony,

Rupert, and Rudolph climbed on and Ernie was up and away to the train wreck again. All the animals were on their way and soon arrived.

Elley and Bob Elephant looked at the engine, and said this will be easy. Bob said "I'll pick up this side of the engine and Elley you push."

Andy Alligator was there too and said, "I'll push too." Several other animals said, "we'll push on the cars." Everybody pushed and the train was back on the tracks real fast.

The engine windows and some of the car windows were dirty. Elley and Bob Elephant said, "We'll take care of that."

Ernie, who was watching too, said "I saw a little lake not far away where you can get water. I'll show you where it is. Hop on guys, you can go too!" Anthony, Rupert, and Rudolph hopped on. Away they went.

Ernie flew low calling out directions to Elley and Bob where the little lake was. They drank a lot of water, hurried back, and squirted it on the window. Hoppity Kangaroo hopped up with some grass in his hands and wiped off the window. Bill and Jerry turned on the sunshine and the cooks got the kitchen going.

Elley and Bob took the tree that fell down off the track. Bill, Jerry, and all of the passengers on the train thanked everybody and the Rabbit Choo Choo, blowing smoke, went right on down the track with cooks cooking delicious carrot celery soup.

Anthony, Rudolph, and Rupert thanked Ernie for all the help. Ernie told them you are very welcome and said, "I'll fly over now and then and check on you guys. I fly high and can see a long way too. It's easy and fun for me. See you!" and Ernie was up and away.

The animals all left too on their way to Nicely Nice Winter Rest Open Hotel Restaurant for a few days spring vacation. Everybody was happy and thanked each other for helping and glad that they were all there and able to help. Everybody felt good.

Rupert, Anthony, and Rudolph stopped at Happy Happy Lake Resort. The train had already gotten there for its three day stay. They saw Bill and Jerry the engineers again. Bill and Jerry thanked them again for helping and were happy everyone was there to help so quickly. Anthony, Rudolph, and Rupert said, "That's okay, that's what friends are for."

Then they found their friend Andy Alligator; he rode down with the train from the train wreck. He had went there for the spring meeting too, but was back to run his ferry service. He took Rupert, Anthony, and Rudolph over to Flower Bug Island because Rupert wanted to see the Twilight Rainbow and the mermaids he had heard about. He had heard they were very beautiful and he wanted to see for himself.

So when twilight came, Anthony and Rudolph made sure they rode the little train. Red, the Flower Bug Island train driver was driving and took them to where the Twilight Rainbow and mermaids could be seen. Rupert was very very happy and wore his cowboy hat all the time.

Then they left Flower Bug Island, thanked Andy Alligator for showing them the island. They said they would tell Ollie Crocodile they met him and that Andy said hello and thank you for sending his friends.

Soon they were back in Rupert's car on their way to Very Best Summer Place.

On the way, they stopped at Chilly Station and Rupert got to see the snow and wear his feather jacket made of yellow duck feathers. They got stuck in almost the same place Anthony did with his car and Jimminy Squirrel and Quickly Rat helped push them out. Anthony gave them some donuts and they were happy. They said they thought Rupert looked nice with his yellow feather jacket and cowboy hat. They had never seen a bullfrog in a nice jacket and hat like that before. Rupert told them thank you. They all said goodbye to their other friends that they had met in the great Hoppity Mountains. Then Rupert sped off in his big car.

They also stopped off in the little town the train passed through on their way to Nicely Nice Winter Rest and showed Rupert Deeply Creepy Cave and the fireflies lighting the lanterns, who had been tired and wanted to rest on the last trip. This time, Terry Turtle told the fireflies if they did not light up, he would tell Tom Beaver the manager and they might lose their jobs. The fireflies said, "okay, okay, okay Terry, we'll rest another time." But they kept mumbling very quietly to themselves that Terry was a grumpy old Turtle and that yeah, yeah, yeah he is.

Terry heard them and said, "Quiet in there you guys."

Then one firefly said, "see, I told you." Then the others sai,d "sshhh sshhh shhh." But this time the lanterns did not go out like before when Anthony and Rudolph went through the cave. The fireflies worked all the way giving light. Everything else was the same in Deepy Creepy Cave.

When they game out Tom Beaver asked how they liked the cave. They told him that they had a nice time.

They were soon back in the car and on their way to the Very Best Summer Place. Then Rupert and Anthony told Rudolph "thank you for a nice vacation. We had a good time."

"You are welcome everybody," said Rudolph.

"You know I heard a story about a sailor in a ship wreck that was in a small boat and saw a little island with a wee small valley. He looked down in the valley and saw a little train with Rabbits driving it and smelled carrot celery soup. He later told others about it, but no one could ever find the place. They told him he must have been out on the water too long and was delirious and out of his mind. He said no, he had seen the place.

Anthony and Rudolph laughed and Rupert laughed too and they said the sailor was right; those folks just don't know. "Say, come to think of it, there was a ship wreck; we saw it on Flower Bug Island."

"Wasn't there" Anthony said.

"Sure was" Rudolph and Rupert said, "we both saw it."

Hey, if you're travelling near Nicely Nicely Summer Place and you see a wee small valley, see smoke and smell carrot celery soup, look close, you just might see the Rabbit Choo Choo passing through.

Bye Bye

About The Author

I'm Al Vicent, originally from Michigan.
I settled in Salinas California after military service
and enjoy writing poetry to fill the vacancy of the
seconds, minutes, and hours that occur during the
days, weeks, months, years.